MONEY MATTERS AFTER 40

A Comprehensive Financial Reboot

By

Nathan Venture. D

To You,

Thank you!

CONTENTS

Introduction: Embracing Financial Reboot After 40

Turning a new leaf in life often comes with its set of anxieties, especially when that turn flips the page to Chapter 40. This milestone is not just a numerical marker but a poignant moment when many start to ponder their legacy—their imprint on the world, and significantly, their financial well-being. Embracing a financial reboot after 40 can feel daunting, yet it's a critical and courageous step towards a future ripe with stability and confidence.

You might be asking yourself, "Is it too late to get my finances in order?" Let's put that worry to rest right away. It's not only possible, but it's also a move that can pivot your life narrative from uncertainty towards one of empowerment and financial clarity. The journey from concern to control starts here, with the right mindset and the tools to carve a path through the thicket of later-life financial planning.

Understanding where you stand is the first stride towards that horizon of financial security. Like mapping a route before a road trip, taking stock of your current financial health illuminates the starting point for your journey. This is about candidly appraising your assets, liabilities, and habits to tailor a plan that's right for you—a critical first stage we delve deeper into as we progress.

Equally paramount is plotting your destination. Setting realistic financial goals gives direction and purpose, conveying a vision for your future that's both hopeful and achievable. These goals act as beacons, guiding your decision-making and providing motivation when the path gets rough—brushing the dust off dreams that may have lain dormant.

The art of budgeting, especially in mid-life, is akin to mastering a dance. It's elegant, rhythmic, and requires constant attention. Crafting a budget that works with your lifestyle can help you achieve harmony between your needs, wants, and dreams. Mid-life brings with it the understanding that a budget isn't a constraint but a means to enrich your life with choices that matter most to you.

As we age, saving takes on new complexity. We balance the urgent need for an emergency cushion with a long-term vision for retirement. The dynamic between short-term and long-term saving strategies is an intricate interplay, each with its unique tempo and time signature. How we save, and where, is a rhythm we'll find together.

Then there's the weight of debt, often a heavy shadow looming over our financial landscapes. Tackling it in your prime years isn't just a challenge; it's a pivotal battle in the war for your financial independence. Paying down this debt—specifically the high-interest kind—frees up not just your finances but your future. It's here that we will equip you with strategies and the steel to avoid the debt traps that ensnare so many.

Investment may come across as a word for the already wealthy, but it's truly the bread and butter of financial growth for us all. Whether it's planting seeds in retirement accounts or navigating the diverse orchard of late-start investments, we will demystify the process, guiding you to make decisions that bear fruit for years to come.

Real estate, be it through ownership or savvy renting decisions, represents a significant cornerstone of post-40 finance. You may be staring down the path of a mortgage or assessing the value of your home's equity. This landscape, while varied, is navigable with the right mindset and information, setting a firm foundation for your financial edifice.

The web of insurance options often appears a labyrinth, winding and complex. But understanding your coverage needs—health, life, and long-term care—brings peace of mind and assurance that you and your loved ones are protected. It's about finding the right thread to follow, leading you safely through the maze.

Retirement planning is not about marking time until an ending; it's about crafting new beginnings—of freedom, purpose, and fulfillment. For the late starter, understanding the unique strategies like catch-up contributions is key. Here, we explore how to grow your nest egg, so it's ready when you are, even if you've felt behind.

Life is replete with uncertainties; one of the few guarantees is change itself. Estate planning ensures your legacy and protects your nearest and dearest when you can't. While the subject might be uncomfortable, establishing wills and trusts allows you to speak for yourself forever, cementing your intentions and love for generations.

Cultivating passive income streams is akin to planting an orchard. It takes patience, care, and time, but the rewards are abundant and long-lasting. Passive income provides a financial harvest that can nourish you well into retirement, offering both freedom and security.

Knowledge is the wellspring of empowerment. Staying attuned to the ever-shifting melody of financial changes and trends is critical. Like any field, the realm of finance is evolving, and continuous education ensures you remain both agile and informed, ready to adapt and make decisions with clarity.

Facing financial hurdles with a lone-wolf approach is an unnecessary heroism. Seeking the counsel of financial advisors is not an admission of defeat, but a strategic alliance. It's about entrusting your journey to a seasoned guide, ensuring that every step you take is measured and advancing you towards your financial summit.

This introduction is just the beginning—it's not the comprehensive financial degree, but it's the orientation to a path that's been waiting for you. Your financial reboot after 40 isn't a backstep; it's a leap forward. It's time to take the reins and steer your financial future towards prosperity, security, and peace of mind, with every subsequent chapter building the foundation. Let's turn this page together, crafting a story of transformation you will be proud to call your own.

CHAPTER 1: UNDERSTANDING YOUR FINANCIAL STARTING POINT

Embarking on a financial journey requires a clear understanding of where you stand. This understanding is not just about knowing your bank balance but taking a comprehensive look at every aspect of your finances. It's time to take a brave step towards scrutinizing your assets, liabilities, income streams, and expenditures to paint a vivid picture of your fiscal reality. This is not the moment for rose-colored glasses; seeing your situation for what it is serves as the foundation for every financial decision you'll make from this point forward. It's imperative to embrace this initial assessment with honesty and without judgment—the sturdier the base, the more resilient your financial future can be. As daunting as it may seem, recognizing your financial baseline is a powerful stride towards setting achievable goals that align with your lifestyle and aspirations, ultimately charting a path for a more secure and confident tomorrow.

Assessing Your Current Financial Health

As you embark on this journey to reinforce your financial foundation, gauging your current financial health is imperative. This assessment acts as a diagnostic tool, revealing areas in your financial life that may need immediate attention or strategic planning. Similar to a medical check-up, this review touches upon various indicators of fiscal wellness and pinpoints strengths to build upon as well as vulnerabilities that require fortification.

To begin, take a comprehensive look at your assets. This isn't just about checking balances in your bank accounts; it encompasses all that you own of value. From retirement accounts to personal property and potential inheritances, understanding what you have is crucial. Be thorough and list out everything – each asset is a building block toward your future financial security.

Next, balance your assets against your liabilities. What you owe – mortgages, car loans, credit card debt, and any other obligations – must be weighed against what you own. If your liabilities overshadow your assets, don't let despair set in. Instead, let that acknowledgement serve as a catalyst for change. You have identified an area with room for growth and improvement.

Income and expenditure analysis follows suit. Track your money's inflow and outflow by scrutinizing bank statements, bills, and receipts. An honest examination of your regular expenses sheds light on your spending habits, often revealing surprises. You may find opportunities to redirect funds away from non-essential spending and towards paying off debt or saving.

Your credit score also plays a pivotal role in your financial health. This three-digit number is more than just a pathway to borrowing; it affects insurance rates, rental opportunities, and much more. A high credit score opens doors while a lower one may limit opportunities. It's essential to know where you stand and take steps to improve or maintain your score.

Insurance coverage is another critical facet. Adequate insurance shields you and your family from unforeseen financial disasters. Assess your health, life, disability, and other insurance policies. Are they appropriate for your current stage in life? Are you over-insured or under-insured? Adjusting your coverage can both save money and prevent catastrophic financial loss in times of crisis.

Emergency funds come next in the sequence of assessment. Can you handle a financial curveball without reaching for a credit card? Your emergency fund should cover several months of living expenses, offering peace of mind and protecting against the need for high-interest debt in tough times.

Retirement planning is not to be overlooked, no matter how far off it seems. Consider what you've already saved and what you're currently contributing towards retirement. Are you taking full advantage of employer-matched funds, if available? Evaluate whether you are on track to retire as wished or if adjustments are needed.

Now, turn your attention to estate documents. It's never too early to plan for the inevitable. Do you have a will or trust established? How about a healthcare directive or power of attorney? These documents help ensure that your wishes are respected, and they provide clear guidance to your loved ones when you're not in a position to do so.

Assessing your tax situation is also essential. Are you effectively managing your tax exposure? Understanding how taxes impact your finances can uncover strategies to minimize what you owe, such as fully utilizing tax-advantaged accounts and deductions.

Continue with scrutinizing your investments. Delve into your portfolio; consider the diversity, risk level, and performance of your investments. At this stage in life, the right investment strategy is critical for balancing growth with risk management.

Lastly, don't overlook your personal relationship with money. Your financial habits, mindset, and emotions about money contribute significantly to your overall financial health. Reflect on past financial decisions and consider how your emotions influenced those choices. Recognizing patterns can help you make better decisions moving forward.

After compiling this information, take a moment to reflect. Recognize the efforts you've already made towards financial stability. This isn't a time for self-judgment but for clarity. With this comprehensive review, you now hold a powerful snapshot of your current financial reality. It's the ground upon which you can build a robust plan towards a financially secure future.

Moving forward, it is vital to regularly revisit and update this assessment. As life's circumstances shift and evolve, so too should your approach to managing your finances. You're not just taking stock of where you are but preparing to navigate towards where you want to be. This assessment is a living document; a testament to your dedication to your financial well-being.

The action you take following this assessment will chart the course for your financial future. Every positive step, no matter how small, is a stride towards greater financial security. With a clear understanding of your current financial health, you are now primed to set realistic goals and create a plan that aligns with your ambitions and your life's unique tapestry.

Setting Realistic Financial Goals

Understanding your financial starting point is essential, but knowing where you're headed is equally important. Setting realistic financial goals is a cornerstone of any solid financial plan, especially for those who are beginning to focus on their financial health later in life. These goals provide direction, motivation, and a sense of purpose.

Firstly, let's define what a realistic financial goal is. It should be Specific, Measurable, Attainable, Relevant, and Time-bound (SMART). Specific goals have a much greater chance of being accomplished than general ones. For instance, instead of just saying you want to save money, decide exactly how much you want to save and by when.

Measurability comes in when you're tracking your progress. Let's say you want to save $10,000 for an emergency fund. Rather than feeling overwhelmed by the total amount, you could measure progress in increments of $1,000. Attainability is about setting goals that are challenging, yet possible. This might mean assessing your current financial situation and recognizing that some sacrifices might have to be made to meet your goal.

To ensure your goals are relevant, they must align with your values and long-term objectives. If owning a home is important to you, then saving for a down payment becomes a relevant goal. Lastly, every goal needs a deadline. Without one, there's little urgency to start working towards the goal now. Time-bound goals help you create short-term milestones on the way to your ultimate aim.

Let's unpack this with an example. Perhaps you've determined that you need to retire with a nest egg of $500,000. Break this down into what you need to save each month, keeping in mind investment returns and the timeframe you have left until retirement. This could mean adjusting your lifestyle or finding ways to increase your income, but it's necessary if you're to meet your target.

Remember to be flexible with your goals. Life can be unpredictable, and your financial plan should be adaptable. If you encounter a setback, don't be discouraged. Assess what's changed, adjust your goals accordingly, and keep moving forward.

With your goals clearly set, you can then create an action plan. This includes identifying steps you need to take immediately, tasks to undertake in the medium term, and what you can do long-term to ensure you reach your desired financial destination. It is about creating a roadmap with actionable waypoints that will guide your journey.

It's common to have multiple financial goals simultaneously. You might be saving for retirement while also setting aside funds for your child's education. While it can seem daunting to tackle several goals at once, the same principles apply: make them SMART, track your progress, and adjust as needed.

Be realistic about the time it takes to achieve significant financial goals. Often, these are not quick wins but the result of persistent effort over many years. It's vital to remain patient and not seek immediate gratification, which can lead to impulsive decisions that depart from your plan.

When setting goals, always consider the potential risks and have mitigation strategies in place. For instance, if you are saving for a long-term goal like retirement, consider the impact of inflation and the necessity of investing your savings to outpace it. If your goal is more immediate, like saving for a down payment on a home, you might choose less volatile savings instruments.

Mental fortitude is part of the journey. It requires you to stay disciplined even when it's tempting to stray from your budget or savings plan. Visualize the peace of mind and satisfaction you'll gain from reaching your goals. Sometimes, this mental image can be a powerful motivator when you're faced with challenges.

Don't forget to celebrate milestones along the way. It's important to recognize and reward yourself for the progress you make. These small celebrations can be incredible morale boosters that rejuvenate your determination to keep pushing toward your ultimate financial goals.

In conclusion, setting realistic financial goals is an integral part of your financial journey, especially in later life. It requires introspection, honesty, planning, and dedication. To ensure success, make your goals smart, trackable, and aligned with your core values. Stay adaptable and remember to acknowledge your achievements along the way. Your financial goals are within reach if you commit to and work systematically towards them.

Chapter 2: The Art of Budgeting Mid-Life

In the prime of life, the canvas of one's financial future still awaits many defining strokes, and it's in Chapter 2—*The Art of Budgeting Mid-Life*—that we begin to paint with purpose. While not every artist begins with the same materials, if you're standing at the midpoint of your journey with an eye toward fiscal responsibility, it's the meticulous blending of discipline and vision that creates a sustainable financial picture. Grasping the brush of budgeting in mid-life means more than simply tracking expenses; it's about delineating between the urgent and the important, forging a plan that allows for both short-term satisfaction and long-term security. It's a process of continuous refinement, where the astute management of one's resources today forms the underpainting for tomorrow's masterpiece. This chapter will guide you with a steady hand, providing the techniques to craft a budget that accommodates both the anticipated and the unforeseen, ensuring that with each stroke, you're not merely surviving, but thriving.

Crafting a Sustainable Budget

As we navigate the midpoint of our lives, it's crucial to craft a budget grounded in sustainability—one that flexes with life's ebbs and flows yet provides a framework sturdy enough to build a secure future upon. This begins with an honest and thorough examination of all income sources, followed by a meticulous itemization of essential and non-essential expenses. Pinpoint where money is genuinely needed versus where it simply wants to go, and you'll uncover opportunities to reallocate funds toward your unshakeable goals. Implementing tools like automated savings and mindful spending tactics can make your budget feel less like an adversary and more like a trusted ally. Remember, adaptive financial habits fostered now, can not only meet today's demands but also carry you confidently into the golden days ahead. A sustainable budget isn't about restriction; it's about making wise choices today that will echo positively in your tomorrows, leading to a mastery of mid-life economics infused with peace of mind.

Prioritizing Expenses and Cutting Costs

This can seem like a challenging mountain to climb, especially when starting later in life. However, with careful planning and dedication, you can scale this financial peak, ensuring a stable and comfortable existence both now and into retirement. This is not about scrimping and saving each penny out of fear, but instead, about empowering yourself to make strategic decisions that will amplify your financial health.

Begin by scrutinizing your expenses with a discerning eye, asking yourself earnestly which of these costs genuinely enrich your life. Needs must come before wants, so secure your housing, utilities, food, health care, and transportation first. Once your essentials are covered, you'll have a clearer view of what's left – this is where you wield your power to cut back.

Turn a critical eye to your subscriptions and memberships. It's alarmingly easy for these monthly payments to slip under the radar, slowly draining resources that could be better utilized elsewhere. Cancel anything that doesn't bring you enough joy or value to justify the cost. By choosing, for example, your favorite streaming service over several you seldom use, you can maintain your enjoyment while cutting costs.

Food expenses can balloon if left unchecked. Eating out frequently or buying lunch every day at work can significantly impact your budget. Start meal planning, and cook at home more often; you'll be surprised by the control this gives you over your diet and finances. Moreover, consider shopping at discount grocers and buying in bulk when appropriate.

Examine your utility usage for opportunities to save. Small changes like reducing your thermostat by a degree or two, turning off lights when you leave a room, or fixing leaky faucets can decrease your bills. You don't have to live uncomfortably to save money, but becoming more energy conscious can make a noticeable difference.

Consolidate and eliminate debt where possible. Particularly, pay attention to high-interest credit cards and loans, aiming to reduce these first. Sometimes, expenses tied to debt are like anchors, weighing down your financial progress. By lessening this burden, you're freeing up money for your future.

Insurance is a must-have, yet that doesn't mean you're stuck with high premiums. Assess your policies and shop around. Remember, as your life changes, so too should your coverage. Ensure you're not paying for more than you need, but also that you have adequate protection for your assets and health.

Creative cost-cutting extends to transportation as well. If you live close to work or amenities, consider walking, biking, or using public transportation instead of driving. This can save you on maintenance, gas, and potentially insurance. If this isn't feasible year-round, even doing so seasonally can have a positive impact on your wallet.

Your home is another place ripe with cost-saving potential. If it's larger than you need or particularly costly to maintain, downsizing might be a practical decision. Lower utility bills, reduced maintenance costs, and perhaps even a smaller mortgage or rent can result from a move to a more appropriately sized living space.

Be smart with your leisure spending. Societal pressure can sometimes lead us into a cycle of costly outings and luxurious vacations. It's certainly important to enjoy life, but there are often less expensive, yet equally fulfilling ways to spend your free time. Explore nature, visit free community events, or learn a new skill through online resources.

Health care expenses often increase with age, making it crucial to find ways to lessen these costs without sacrificing quality of care. Make sure you're using the benefits you're entitled to, and look into supplemental programs that can assist with premiums or out-of-pocket costs.

Sometimes, generating additional income can be more effective than cutting costs. Consider monetizing a hobby, seeking part-time work, or selling unused items. Every extra dollar can be directed towards savings, investing, or reducing debt further accelerating your financial objectives.

Communication services, like your internet and cell phone plans, have become essentials in the modern world, yet they can also be a source of savings. Evaluate your usage and downsize your plan if you consistently use less than you're paying for. Alternatively, if you're overpaying due to constant overages, a slightly higher plan could be more economical in the long run.

Reflect on your shopping habits. Impulse buys can add up, leaving you with a hole in your budget and, often, items you don't genuinely need. Make lists before you shop and stick to them. By doing so, you'll resist the temptation of unnecessary purchases and keep your finances on track.

Lastly, remember that every small effort counts. By prudently reviewing your monthly expenditures and tweaking your habits, you can steadily work towards increased financial flexibility. Prioritizing expenses and cutting costs isn't just a one-time effort—it's a continuous process that, when attended to diligently, can lead to a future of fiscal certainty and comfort.

Imagine the peace that comes with knowing your finances are secure, a tranquility born from making informed and thoughtful choices about where your money goes. This isn't just a dream reserved for the thrifty few; it's a reality within your reach. With each step you take in prioritizing expenses and cutting costs, you're crafting a stable and promising financial future for yourself and your loved ones.

Monitoring and Adjusting Your Budget

Having crafted a sensible budget, you've taken a crucial step towards financial stability in mid-life. It's essential, however, to understand that a budget isn't set in stone. As life unfolds, your budget must evolve, adapt, and respond to the changes—both expected and unforeseen. Monitoring and adjusting your budget will determine its effectiveness and your success.

Think of your budget as a living document, one that requires regular reviews. It's not uncommon for expenses to fluctuate; a vigilant eye can detect patterns or inconsistencies, allowing for swift adjustments. If a particular category in your budget consistently overshoots, it may be time to reassess your limits or find ways to cut back.

Similarly, income isn't static. Perhaps you've taken on a part-time job, received a pay raise, or started a new side hustle. This welcome increase should be accounted for by reassessing your savings or investment strategies within your budget, ensuring these extra funds are put to good use.

Keep track of large, infrequent expenses such as property taxes, insurance premiums or maintenance costs. These could potentially derail your budget if not planned for. Considering these expenses as monthly costs by setting aside a portion each month can mitigate surprise financial burdens.

The process of monitoring your budget also involves examining your financial goals. Goals set earlier may need refinement. If you've accomplished a goal, celebrate your success but then promptly set a new one to keep your financial growth on an upward trajectory. Your budget should reflect these evolving goals.

Adaptability is key when unexpected life events occur—whether it's a job loss, health emergency, or a sudden home repair. Your budget should provide a measure of flexibility for you to navigate through these rough patches without incurring debt or jeopardizing your long-term financial well-being.

One way to ensure flexibility is by maintaining an emergency fund. While this is a topic addressed in its own chapter, it's worth noting that an emergency fund is a dynamic aspect of your budget that needs regular assessment and adjustment based on your current life situation.

Regular budget meetings, monthly or quarterly, are crucial. These check-ins provide the opportunity for you to review receipts, account statements, and other financial documents to confirm that you are on track. If you discover any discrepancies or oversights, you can address them promptly.

Technological aids can be immensely helpful. Numerous apps and software are available to assist in tracking your spending and can alert you when you're approaching your budget limits. Sometimes, all it takes to avoid overspending is a real-time reminder that you're near your threshold.

Adjusting your budget also means negotiating with yourself and your family members. When cuts are needed, deciding where and how much requires open communication and sometimes, difficult choices. Always aim for choices that stabilize your mid-life financial trajectory, even if they require short-term sacrifices.

Don't overlook the psychological aspect of budgeting. It's common to experience frustration or discouragement if things don't align immediately. However, it's the commitment to regular monitoring and adjustment that breeds long-term success. Each review should be approached with optimism and the resolve to do better, not with self-criticism.

Social events, vacations, and holidays are often budgeting pain points that necessitate a proactive approach. Instead of letting these occasions strain your finances, anticipate and plan for them within your budget, setting aside funds incrementally to alleviate the financial pressure when they occur.

Lastly, it's wise to document your budget adjustments. Keeping a log allows you to analyze your financial decision-making over time, offering insights into what strategies work best for you. This documentation can serve as a motivational tool, visibly demonstrating your progress and mastery over your personal finances.

Remember, the mid-life stage offers its own set of financial challenges and opportunities. Embracing the process of budget monitoring and adjustment ensures that you're not just reacting to life's financial demands, but actively managing and improving your fiscal health with intention and foresight. Stay committed to the art of budgeting, for it is one of the most potent tools in securing your financial future.

By treating your budget less like a final edict and more like a guideline, you open the door to financial resilience and adaptability. As you advance through the subsequent chapters, bear in mind that each component of your financial plan is interdependent—your ability to save, invest, tackle debt, and plan for retirement is predicated on the fluidity and precision of your budgeting practices.

CHAPTER 3: THE ESSENTIALS OF SAVING AFTER 40

As life briskly moves us through our forties and beyond, the principles of saving take on new dimensions, compelling us to confront the urgency of time with a steadfast resolve. This chapter carves into the essentials of cushioning our future selves, beginning with the non-negotiables—fortifying an emergency fund to navigate life's unpredicted currents. While we will delve deeper into the intricate balance between short-term and long-term saving strategies later, it's vital to understand that post-40, the essence of saving isn't merely about stockpiling cash but about crafting a resilient foundation for the impending chapters of life. Crafted intentionally, savings become the silent guardians of our peace of mind, averting financial disarray that can all too easily upend the stability we've painstakingly built. Distinguishing between immediate needs and evolving life goals, saving in these prime years involves a keen eye for balance and a commitment to consistency, ensuring that each dollar saved today is a step towards the sanctity of secure golden years.

Establishing Emergency Funds

As we delve into the crux of savings post-40, the cornerstone of a solid financial foundation often begins with establishing an emergency fund. There's a prevailing sense of urgency that accompanies the realization that the buffer for unexpected financial shocks isn't as robust as it should be. The journey of a thousand miles begins with a single step, so let's explore why and how to build that all-important emergency reserve.

The purpose of an emergency fund is unmistakable: it's a financial lifeline during unexpected events. Unforeseen medical bills, sudden job loss, or urgent home repairs can be destabilizing when you're caught unprepared. The foresight to establish an emergency fund transforms panic into peace of mind when life throws you a curveball.

But how much is enough? Conventional wisdom recommends having three to six months' worth of living expenses in your emergency account. However, after the age of 40, aiming towards the higher end of this spectrum—or even beyond—is prudent. Aging brings with it an increased likelihood of health issues, job market volatility, and other unpredictable costs, and your emergency fund needs to reflect this reality.

Where to start, then? Begin with a precise assessment of your monthly expenses—housing, food, transportation, and other necessities—and multiply this figure by six. This will yield your six-month expense coverage target. If this figure seems daunting, don't despair. The key is to start small and build consistently over time.

To accumulate this reserve, open a dedicated savings account that's easily accessible yet separate from your regular checking account to resist the temptation of dipping into it for non-emergencies. Opt for high-yield savings accounts or money market accounts which offer slightly better interest rates to inflate your fund more effectively.

Initiate the process by setting up an automatic transfer to your emergency fund immediately after each paycheck is deposited. Even a modest amount between $50 to $100 can kickstart your fund. Treat it as a non-negotiable expense in your monthly budget, similar to rent or a mortgage payment.

It's important to periodically review the growth of your emergency fund and adjust contributions as needed. This is especially true after any significant life changes, such as a raise in income, a decrease in expenses, or after a large withdrawal from the fund to cover an emergency. The goal is to always be rebuilding and ensuring the fund's size is current with your lifestyle and expenses.

Remember, however, that the emergency fund isn't an investment; it's insurance. The primary goal isn't to achieve high returns, but rather to be a reliable, liquid asset. Therefore, while your fund should be earning some interest, its accessibility in times of crisis is paramount.

There may be times when you're tempted to use these funds for opportunities that seem pressing, such as investing in a lucrative deal or taking advantage of a sale. It's critical to resist these impulses. The emergency fund isn't for opportunities; it's for emergencies. By staying disciplined, you ensure the fund serves its purpose.

For those starting later in life, the urgency for an emergency fund cannot be overstated, and neither can the sense of accomplishment that comes with achieving this milestone. A well-furnished emergency fund will not just insulate you from the financial surprises that life may throw your way but also imbue you with confidence and a sense of security.

The psychological benefits of having an emergency fund are not to be understated. Stress and worry about the future can be significantly mitigated by the knowledge that you have a buffer. This peace of mind allows you to focus on other aspects of your financial journey, like paying off debt, investing for retirement, and planning for long-term goals.

Furthermore, in our 40s and beyond, we often find ourselves sandwiched between the needs of aging parents and our own children's education or career beginnings. An emergency fund can provide the flexibility and resource to manage these generational pressures without derailing our own financial path.

If, at any point, you've had to dip into your fund, once the emergency has passed, make replenishing it a priority. You've seen its worth in action, and knowing it's there and fully stocked will help carry you through the next unexpected event with grace and stability.

Lastly, don't be discouraged if progress seems slow at times. The act of saving is itself an assurance that you're working towards greater financial stability. Each deposit is a step towards not only securing your now but also safeguarding your future.

Building and maintaining your emergency fund is an ongoing process. It's part of a lifelong commitment to financial responsibility and resilience. Whether just starting to focus on your savings or fine-tuning your approach in your prime years, regard your emergency reserve as an indispensable component of your financial well-being. It's the cushion that can soften life's blows, allowing you to rebound and move forward with determination and a clear mind.

Short-Term vs. Long-Term Savings Strategies

Embarking on the journey of saving after 40 presents a unique set of challenges and opportunities. One key dimension to navigate is the distinction between short-term and long-term savings strategies. While both are crucial in a well-rounded financial plan, understanding their respective roles can lead to a more secure and comfortable future.

Short-term savings are essentially your financial safety net. They provide the buffer you need to absorb life's unexpected costs without disrupting your financial stability. This could range from an unforeseen car repair to a last-minute travel expense. By setting aside a portion of your income into an accessible savings account, you're not only preparing for emergencies but also avoiding the need to take on debt when unplanned expenses arise.

Long-term savings, on the other hand, are the backbone of your future financial independence. These are savings that you invest with the intent of not touching for many years, such as retirement funds or savings for major life goals, like buying a house. Long-term savings may involve investing in the stock market, bonds, or other financial instruments that offer the potential for higher returns over time.

To achieve a sustainable short-term savings plan, start by evaluating your monthly income and expenses. Identify areas where you can cut back and redirect that cash to your savings. The golden rule is to save at least three to six months' worth of living expenses in an easily accessible savings account. This cushion will help you weather storms without derailing your long-term goals.

When it comes to long-term savings, it's important to consider the effects of inflation and the time value of money. Your dollar today will not have the same purchasing power in 20 years. That's why investments that may offer higher returns, despite their risks, are worth considering for long-term growth. It's all about balancing risk and reward to achieve your future financial objectives.

One critical element in short-term savings is discipline. Setting up automatic transfers to a designated savings account can eliminate the temptation to spend that money. Treat your savings like a bill that must be paid. This automation ensures that your safety net is continuously growing.

Long-term savings strategies often include tax-advantaged retirement accounts like IRAs and 401(k)s. If you're over 40, the IRS allows for catch-up contributions, which means you can put away more money than younger savers. Leveraging these accounts can significantly enhance your nest egg by the time you retire.

The key difference between short-term and long-term savings also lies in where you keep your money. Short-term savings need to be readily accessible, so high-yield savings accounts or money market accounts are suitable options. They offer better interest rates than traditional savings accounts, making sure your money isn't entirely idle.

For long-term savings, diversification is your friend. A mix of stocks, bonds, and other investment assets can help protect against market volatility and provide growth opportunities. The idea is to achieve a balance that aligns with your risk tolerance and financial goals as you move closer to retirement.

Remember that it's never too late to start saving, but the sooner you begin, the more benefit you reap from compounding interest and market gains. If you're just getting started after 40, focus on ramping up your long-term savings quickly while still maintaining a healthy short-term reserve.

Short-term savings goals should be reviewed and adjusted annually as your life circumstances change, ensuring that your safety net is always robust enough to cover your current lifestyle. Long-term savings, while reviewed less frequently, should still be monitored to make any needed adjustments based on the performance of your investments or changes in your retirement goals.

While you're working hard to build your short-term savings, don't let it derail your long-term objectives. One should not come at the high cost of the other. Instead, they need to complement each other. Having a clear picture of your financial landscape allows you to allocate funds effectively between short and long-term savings.

Implementing a laddered savings strategy can also be beneficial. This involves having a series of savings accounts or CDs with different maturity dates. As each matures, you have the option to re-invest in a long-term vehicle or replenish your short-term funds, depending on your current needs and market conditions.

Finally, let's acknowledge that motivation can wane, especially when it comes to long-term savings. To stay on track, visualize your retirement, the travels, the leisure time, or the ability to help your loved ones. This vision can be a powerful motivator to keep contributing to those long-term savings accounts, even when it feels like retirement is still a long way off.

In summary, striking the right balance between short-term and long-term savings strategies is vital for building a secure financial future after 40. It requires thoughtful planning, committed execution, and regular reviews and adjustments to ensure both immediate needs and future dreams are within reach. With diligence and determination, you can create a robust financial safety net while steadily moving towards your long-term aspirations.

CHAPTER 4: TACKLING DEBT IN YOUR PRIME YEARS

As you stride into the thick of your prime years, the importance of addressing your debts head-on can't be overstated. Within these years, the strength of your financial foundation hinges on the strategic maneuvers you make to reduce and eradicate outstanding debts. It's a period ripe for action; a time when you must prioritize repayments, while balancing the necessity of savings and the inevitability of daily expenses. Here we're not just moving numbers, we're setting the stage for a financial resurgence. Imagine looking at your balance sheet and watching debt figures dwindle, replaced by growing assets: this is your future, within reach. As daunting as it may seem, there's a pragmatic vibrancy in developing a targeted plan to tackle high-interest debt first – it's like severing the most tangled ropes to watch your financial sails billow with promise. While avoiding new debt is crucial, focus on making informed, disciplined choices that align with a life free from the anchors of past financial burdens. By employing proven strategies and maintaining a course that ensures you avoid common debt traps, the prime years of your life become not only a testament to your resilience but a beacon to a secure, unwavering financial future.

Strategies for Paying Down Debt

Embarking on the journey to financial liberation, especially in the thick of your prime years, begins with dismantling the barriers of debt. A strategic approach to this, one that beckons the promise of a lighter tomorrow, involves first pinpointing those debts that gnaw away at your resources with high interest—the notorious budget drainers. Facing these head-on allows for a shift in momentum, paving the way for more substantial victories as smaller debts subsequently fall like dominos. This method, often known as the avalanche approach, prioritizes debts in descending order of their interest rates and can be a powerful tool in your financial arsenal. Consistency becomes your ally here; regular payments above the minimum can vastly accelerate the retirement of your debt. Additionally, consolidating multiple debts into one lower-interest payment streamlines the process, potentially reducing stress and granting clarity as you chart your progress. Remember, the goal is not only to reduce what you owe, but to rebuild the robust financial foundation upon which your future stability rests. Every dollar that frees itself from the clutches of debt is an investment in that brighter, more secure tomorrow.

High-Interest Debt Reduction Techniques

When we talk about climbing out of debt in the prime years of life, there is a certain type of debt that hangs over our finances like a storm cloud: high-interest debt. It's oppressive, it's persistent, and it can inhibit our financial progress with its steep interest rates. Often, this includes credit card debt, payday loans, and certain personal loans. Reducing high-interest debt can feel like an uphill battle, but with a few strategic moves, one can make definitive progress toward financial liberation.

Before diving into techniques, let's establish a primary approach: target high-interest rates first. The reason is simple; these debts cost the most over time. It's not just about the dollar amount you borrowed; it's also about how much it will cost you if you let it sit. There are various strategies one can employ to tackle high-interest debt, and we will explore some of the most effective ones.

One popular method is the debt avalanche technique. This involves making minimum payments on all your debts except for the one with the highest interest rate, which you'll concentrate extra payments on. Once that's paid off, you move on to the debt with the next highest rate, and so on. This method can be incredibly effective in reducing the total amount of interest you pay over time.

In situations where motivation is just as important as methodology, the debt snowball method can be beneficial. Unlike the avalanche, the snowball method focuses on paying off the smallest debts first, regardless of interest rate. This 'quick win' approach can boost your motivation, keeping you on track with your debt reduction journey. However, it may cost you a bit more in interest over time compared to the avalanche approach.

Another technique worth considering is applying for a balance transfer credit card with a 0% introductory APR offer. Transferring high-interest credit card balances to such a card can provide a window of opportunity where your balance isn't growing due to interest, which allows you to pay down the principal balance more effectively.

Consolidating multiple debts into a single, lower-interest loan can also simplify your payments and reduce the amount of interest you'll pay. However, it's critical to assess any fees associated with consolidation and ensure that the new loan indeed has more favorable terms.

There are more aggressive strategies, too, like negotiating with creditors. It's possible to negotiate a lower interest rate or a settlement for less than what you owe, although this can have repercussions for your credit score. If you choose this route, it may be wise to seek professional advice to navigate the negotiations safely.

Adjusting your budget to find extra money for debt repayment is equally important. Scrutinizing your spending and cutting back on non-essentials can free up funds that can be allocated towards paying down high-interest debt.

Increasing income, whether through a side job, selling unused items, or seeking a raise at work, can provide extra funds to apply towards debt. The more you can put towards your debt, the faster you'll see progress.

It's important, too, to keep a close watch on your credit report and score as you work to pay down debt. Good credit can open the door to lower-interest loan options in the future, which can assist in debt management.

Creating a debt reduction plan that is realistic and sustainable is critical. Set clear goals, track your progress, and adjust as needed. Acknowledge that setbacks may occur, but the key is consistency and the determination to continue moving forward.

To keep the momentum, celebrate small victories. Each time you pay off a balance, give yourself recognition for your hard work. This positive reinforcement can inspire continued effort and help maintain your focus on the ultimate goal of debt freedom.

Finally, maintain open communication with family members about debt reduction goals and strategies. Support from loved ones can be essential, and working together can create a stronger front against debt.

In the atmosphere of debt reduction, it's easy to become discouraged or overwhelmed. However, it's crucial to stay informed about the tools and techniques at your disposal. Remember, taking control of high-interest debt is a significant step towards financial stability and freedom.

The journey towards reducing high-interest debt is not just a financial challenge; it's an emotional and psychological one as well. Stay committed, be patient with yourself, and adopt a forward-thinking perspective. With smart strategies and a consistent approach, you can overcome high-interest debt and set a course for a brighter, more secure financial future.

Your golden years should be a time for enjoying the fruits of your labor, not struggling with the chains of past debt. With these high-interest debt reduction techniques, you have the knowledge to break free and pave the way to a comfortable and secure retirement. Take that first step today, and transform your tomorrow.

Avoiding Common Debt Traps

In the prime years of your financial journey, vigilance is key – especially when it comes to avoiding the pitfalls that can exacerbate debt. An array of common traps are ever-present, waiting to ensnare the unwary. Understanding these pitfalls and learning how to sidestep them can bolster your financial resilience significantly. Let's delve into the tactics and foresight required to steer clear of these potential setbacks.

Firstly, credit card debt is a habitual offender in the realm of financial traps. The convenience and immediacy that credit cards offer can be deceptive, leading to a slippery slope of high interest and ever-growing balances. To avoid this snare, treat credit cards with respect and caution. Pay off balances in full each month, if possible, to forgo interest charges, and resist the urge to spend beyond your means.

Another trap that often catches individuals off guard is the lure of payday loans. Appearing as a quick fix to cash flow issues, these loans are notorious for their astronomical interest rates and can lead to a cycle of debt that's hard to escape. Instead, build an emergency fund for unexpected expenses; even small, regular savings contributions can create a buffer to protect you from turning to such precarious options.

Auto loans are yet another area where debt can quickly escalate. The temptation of driving a new or more luxurious vehicle can lead to extended payment terms and higher interest costs. Before signing a lengthy loan agreement, consider the long-term impact on your budget and explore more affordable vehicle options that won't hinder your financial goals.

When discussing ways to elude debt traps, we can't overlook the subtle pull of store financing and "buy now, pay later" schemes. These offers can make large purchases seem manageable but often come with high-interest rates after an initial promotional period. Read the fine print and be wary of any financing that will balloon your cost over time.

Mortgages, while typically considered "good debt," can also become a pitfall if not managed with prudence. Overextending on a home purchase or refinancing to tap equity for non-essential expenses can jeopardize your financial stability. Ensure your home payment is within your budget and that you're not using your home as an ATM for discretionary spending.

Subscription services, though individually small amounts, can accumulate and contribute to debt when not monitored. Regularly review your subscriptions and cut out those that aren't essential or that you no longer use. Small savings here can add up and help keep your debt in check.

Minimum payments on debts present another understated trap. Paying only the minimum prolongs your debt and results in a higher overall payment due to interest. Aim to pay more than the minimum, especially on high-interest debt, to reduce balances quicker and save on interest payments.

Medical debt, often unexpected, can be particularly damaging. To minimize the risk, make sure you have appropriate health insurance coverage and understand your benefits. Negotiate payment plans with healthcare providers and hospitals before debt goes to collection to avoid a negative impact on your credit.

Lastly, the trap of inaction or denial must be addressed. Ignoring your debt won't make it disappear; it will likely grow more daunting. This means prioritizing debt reduction, regularly reviewing your financial plan, and making adjustments as necessary.

In the fight against debt, knowledge is power. Educate yourself on the various debt-relief strategies available to you, such as debt consolidation or negotiation, and when these might be appropriate. Remember that taking proactive steps, rather than reactive measures, sets the foundation for a debt-free future.

Understanding the psychological aspect of spending is important as well. Reflect on your spending triggers and habits. Are you shopping out of emotion, such as stress or boredom? Recognizing these patterns can help you curb unnecessary spending and direct that money towards paying down debt instead.

Communication is also critical in the realm of financial health. If you share finances with a spouse or partner, maintain an open dialogue to ensure you're aligned on your financial goals and approaches to managing debt. Miscommunication can lead to duplicate spending or conflicting financial strategies, which can sabotage debt-reduction efforts.

To consolidate your learning and remain firm in your resolve, consider joining personal finance groups, either locally or online. Engaging with like-minded individuals committed to improving their financial situation can provide support, accountability, and shared wisdom as you work to escape the common traps of debt.

As you navigate through your prime earning years, remember that financial stability isn't just about making money – it's about making wise decisions with the money you have. It's about sidestepping common debt traps and approaching your finances with a combination of strategic thinking, disciplined budgeting, and forward planning. Your future self will thank you for the foresight and self-restraint exercised during these crucial years.

Remain vigilant, stay informed, and above all, keep a close eye on the roadmap of your financial journey. With each trap you avoid, you move closer to the ultimate destination: a life of financial security and the freedom that comes with it. The pathway to a stable financial future is not beyond reach; it's a matter of smart choices and steadfast commitment to your financial well-being.

CHAPTER 5: INVESTING WISELY AT A LATER STAGE

Transitioning into the heart of our journey, we recognize that investing isn't just for the youthful go-getters; it's a pivotal part of securing a stable future for those who've weathered a few more seasons. In the canvas of life's second act, where experience colors our decisions, choosing to invest wisely takes on a profound importance. While some might think timing has slipped away, this chapter stands as a beacon of opportunity, illustrating that it's never too late to harness the power of the market. We're going to delve into the essentials of tailoring an investment portfolio that balances risk with reward, aligning with the unique considerations that come with these enriched chapters in life.

Without the luxury of decades to recover from missteps, we must craft a strategy that accounts for a shorter time horizon yet still brims with potential for growth. We'll explore how to optimize retirement accounts, making use of IRAs and 401(k) plans designed with the late-starter in mind. Here, annuities also come into play, presenting a tool for guaranteed income amidst a landscape of uncertainty. With eyes wide open to the risks, yet sights set unfalteringly on our goals, we'll lay the groundwork for investments that mature as gracefully as we have. It's about making informed choices, embracing the wisdom of diversification, and growing our wealth with both care and courage. So let's press onward, mindful that with each wise investment, the seeds of a secure and fruitful retirement are sown.

Understanding Investment Fundamentals

As we navigate the waters of financial security, understanding the core principles of investing becomes increasingly vital, especially when orchestrating our financial symphony later in life. The cornerstone of prudent investing is grasping the nature of stocks, bonds, mutual funds, and other investment vehicles. Let's embark upon unraveling these concepts with clarity and purpose, ensuring you can make informed decisions aligned with your financial aspirations.

Starting with the basics, stocks represent ownership in companies, and when you purchase a stock, you're buying a piece of that company's future profits and growth. While they can provide substantial returns, stocks are often volatile, which means the value can rise and fall based on market conditions, company performance, and other factors. Diversifying your stock portfolio across various industries and companies can mitigate this risk, positioning you for steadier growth over time.

Bonds, on the other hand, are akin to loans given to corporations or government entities. When you buy a bond, you're lending money in exchange for periodic interest payments and the return of the bond's face value at maturity. Bonds are generally considered safer than stocks but offer lower returns, providing a ballast to your investment portfolio in choppy financial seas.

Mutual funds are investment vehicles that pool money from many investors to purchase a diversified portfolio of stocks, bonds, or other securities. Managed by a professional, these funds offer diversification and professional management, making them a compelling option for those who prefer a hands-off approach to their investments.

Understanding the relationship between risk and return is paramount. Investments with the potential for higher returns often come with higher risk. This is where your individual risk tolerance comes into play - how much fluctuation in investment value you're comfortable with based on your financial situation and time horizon. That comfort level will guide your investment choices and asset allocation, balancing potential gains with the peace of mind you crave.

It's essential to consider the impact of fees and taxes on your investment returns. Fees can reduce your earnings significantly over time, so choosing investment options with lower expense ratios is wise. And since taxes can also take a bite out of your gains, understanding tax-efficient investing strategies, such as utilizing retirement accounts or choosing tax-efficient funds, will serve your bottom line well.

A concept often overlooked but vital in the investment world is the power of compounding. Compounding occurs when your investment earnings generate their own earnings. Given time, this can turn modest savings into considerable wealth, making it an investor's best friend. As a late-stage investor, maximizing your contributions to take full advantage of compounding is a strategy that can help catch up on building your nest egg.

Don't be swayed by the ebb and flow of market trends and noise; instead, focus on setting a long-term investment strategy. Fluctuations in the market are normal, but a well-thought-out plan based on sound investment principles will keep you anchored to your financial goals. This strategy might include a consistent investment schedule, known as dollar-cost averaging, to help smooth out the effects of market volatility.

Asset allocation is another critical concept that refers to the way you spread your investments across different asset categories. The right mix of stocks, bonds, and cash equivalents can help you manage investment risks. Periodically revisiting and rebalancing your asset allocation to align with your changing risk tolerance and financial goals is key to maintaining a fluid and effective investing strategy.

It's worth emphasizing the importance of patience in investing. Success doesn't usually happen overnight. By staying committed to your investment strategy and staying the course even during market downturns, you fortify your future financial health. Remember, it's time in the market, not timing the market, that typically yields the most favorable results.

While investing can seem complex, focusing on one element at a time can make the process approachable and manageable. Start by getting familiar with investment terms, how different assets function, how they fit within your overall financial plan, and how they correlate with the risks you are willing to take. With knowledge comes confidence, and with confidence, the ability to make wise investment choices increases.

Remember that diversification is your shield—a way to spread risk across various investments to cushion against losses in any one area. It's putting your eggs in multiple baskets so that you have others to rely on should one fall. Diversify not only across different asset classes but also within those classes, and even geographically by investing internationally.

Investing wisely at this stage also means recognizing the importance of keeping an emergency fund outside of your investments. Life's unpredictability doesn't retire, and having funds for unexpected expenses helps to ensure you won't need to liquidate investments at an inopportune time, which can derail your investment strategy.

Now that you have a foundation of investment knowledge, you're at the helm of your financial ship, equipped to chart a course towards a thriving retirement. It's your foresight, discipline, and commitment to learning that will amplify your financial acumen, allowing you to capitalize on opportunities and navigate the inevitable challenges with grace and poise.

Educating yourself on investment fundamentals is a continuous journey, much like any other aspect of self-improvement. With your newfound understanding, you're prepared to delve deeper into retirement accounts and late-start investments, which will be the next vital steps in fortifying your future financial freedom.

Retirement Accounts and Late-Start Investments

Embarking on the investment journey later in life can feel daunting, but the world of retirement accounts is brimming with opportunities for those who are willing to take the plunge. Starting to invest in your retirement may not have the early starter's advantage, but it's far from a lost cause, especially with vehicles like IRAs and 401(k)s that offer tax advantages designed to bolster your golden years. Allocating funds into these accounts can significantly impact your long-term savings. Supplement these with annuities for predictable income and you're crafting a diverse retirement portfolio to rely on. Moreover, it's the time to harness the power of catch-up contributions, a powerful feature that allows individuals over 50 to surpass regular contribution limits, accelerating retirement savings when it matters most. The aim is clear: maximize your assets, minimize taxes, and fortify your later years with confidence and financial peace of mind.

IRAs, 401(k)s, and Annuities

As individuals look to strengthen their financial footing later in life, understanding the vehicles that promote retirement savings is crucial. IRAs, 401(k)s, and annuities, each offer distinctive advantages and opportunities that align with different retirement strategies. Let's dive deep into these instruments, and uncover how they can fortify your financial future even if you find yourself embarking on this journey later than many others.

Individual Retirement Accounts, or IRAs, serve as a foundational building block for retirement savings. Traditional IRAs allow you to contribute pre-tax earnings, which may help lower your taxable income now, while the investments grow tax-deferred. Withdrawals during retirement are then taxed as ordinary income. On the flip side, Roth IRAs are funded with after-tax dollars, permitting tax-free growth and withdrawals under qualifying circumstances. This type of account can be particularly strategic if you expect to be in a higher tax bracket during retirement or seek tax diversification.

For those employed by organizations that offer 401(k) plans, these employer-sponsored plans can be a powerful tool in your arsenal. Contributions to 401(k)s are commonly made pre-tax, reducing your current taxable income and providing tax-deferred growth. Many employers also match a portion of your contributions, essentially granting free money towards your retirement objectives. For those over 50, catch-up contributions are an additional feature allowing for accelerated saving.

Annuities are yet another avenue, offering a unique blend of investment and insurance. Purchased from a financial institution, annuities promise to pay out a steady stream of income over time, providing a safeguard against outliving your assets. Generally, there are three types: fixed, variable, and indexed annuities, each with its own risk profile and payout method. Annuities can supplement your retirement plan, especially if you seek predictable, guaranteed income.

What's essential to grasp is that these retirement vehicles aren't mutually exclusive. An informed approach often involves a combination of IRAs, 401(k)s, as well as annuities, to create a well-rounded, diversified retirement portfolio. To make the most of these tools, one must step beyond the comfortable and acquaint themselves with the particulars of each option.

When contemplating Traditional IRA contributions, bear in mind the current tax benefits juxtaposed with the future tax responsibilities. If you project that your retirement tax rate will be lower than your current rate, the upfront tax deductions of a Traditional IRA can make a lot of financial sense. However, if you're more optimistic about your future financial status, the Roth IRA's tax-free growth might shine as the superior path.

In the realm of 401(k)s, you'll encounter two primary versions – traditional and Roth. For the traditional 401(k), similar to the IRA, taxes on contributions are deferred until withdrawal, offering a semblance of immediate tax relief. With a Roth 401(k), as with a Roth IRA, you pay taxes on the contributions upfront, enabling tax-free accumulation and withdrawal of the funds later, provided certain conditions are met. The choice between the two often hinges on current versus anticipated retirement tax rates.

And so, as you navigate these decisions, consider the flexibility and potential penalties associated with each option. Traditional IRAs and 401(k)s impose required minimum distributions starting at age 72, with penalties for failure to withdraw the correct amounts. Roth IRAs offer more adaptability, with no required minimum distributions during the owner's lifetime, which can significantly affect your retirement planning and tax situation.

The journey towards a serene retirement isn't simply about stashing away funds; it's about crafting a tapestry of finances that respects your current life, anticipates your future needs, and mitigates uncertainties. Annuities, for many, are the threads that provide the stability of income, reducing the anxiety of market volatility and the fear of assets depletion.

Moreover, when examining annuities, it's vital to be aware of their fees and the implications of their guarantees. Fixed annuities usually offer lower returns but come with the solace of stable payouts. Variable annuities, while tied to investment portfolios with the potential for higher returns, carry greater risk and often higher fees.

Indexed annuities strike a balance, offering returns linked to a market index but with certain protections against loss.

Deciding which combination of these retirement vehicles is best for you can seem daunting. This is where the value of proactive planning and continued education comes into sharp relief. Understanding the tax implications, the growth potential, and the associated risks of your investments positions you to make informed decisions that resonate with your personal financial ethos.

As we move forward, remember, it's never too late—or too early—to align your financial strategies with your retirement aspirations. Your next step is to put in the time to comprehend the nuances of IRAs, 401(k)s, and annuities. Equipped with this knowledge, you're embarking on a journey not just to retirement, but to financial freedom and certainty in your golden years.

Life can be unpredictable, and one's financial journey is rarely a linear path. But with a grasp on the instruments available and a determination to strategically plan for the future, achieving a securely funded retirement is wholly possible, even for those who consider themselves late bloomers in the realm of financial planning.

Taking the reins of your retirement planning with an informed and purposeful mindset ensures that each step you take is one step closer to the future you envision. With attention, diligence, and resolve, the rewards of a comfortable and self-reliant retirement are within your grasp.

The narrative of your financial future starts with you. Your actions today can transform the uncertainty of tomorrow into a foundation of stability and confidence. Embrace these powerful tools, engage with them, and let them guide you towards the outcomes you deserve.

Ultimately, IRAs, 401(k)s, and annuities are more than mere investment terms; they are vessels steering you towards prosperity. Let them lift you above the tides of doubt and escalate you to new heights of financial well-being. Your later years can be defined not by regret or chance, but by the richness of choice and the joy of fulfillment.

CHAPTER 6: THE BASICS OF REAL ESTATE AND HOME OWNERSHIP

As you've started to fortify your finances, it's essential to navigate the foundational aspects of real estate and home ownership — a pillar for many in their pursuit of financial stability later in life. Understanding the nuance between buying and renting can make a significant difference in your long-term net worth. It's not simply about having a roof over your head, but making an informed decision that complements your retirement plan and suits your lifestyle. Grasping the ins and outs of mortgages will allow you to manage debt smartly, tapping into equity while avoiding financial strain. In this chapter, you'll learn how to discern what type of housing arrangement aligns with your goals, how to utilize your home as a financial asset, and the importance of building equity that can bolster your security as you advance towards retirement.

Deciding to Buy or Rent in Later Life

Entering the latter chapters of life comes with thoughtful considerations, especially when it comes to your living situation. The decision between renting and purchasing a home is pivotal, and it bears different weights at this stage than it did in your earlier years. While buying a home might seem like the culmination of the American dream, renting can often offer flexibility and freedom that align with changing lifestyles and needs. Let's unravel this complex decision-making cloth one thread at a time.

Firstly, it's crucial to reflect on your current financial health, the very matter you've likely been cultivating and nurturing throughout the previous chapters. Owning a home could potentially offer long-term financial benefits, such as building equity and gaining capital appreciation. However, the initial costs of home buying, including the down payment, closing costs, and any immediate home repairs, can be considerable. If you've successfully established a robust financial foundation and have the savings to cover these upfront costs, buying might be within your reach.

Conversely, renting may be more in tune with a lifestyle seeking less responsibility and more liquidity. Renting doesn't tie you up with a mortgage, freeing up your budget for other investments that could generate returns more aligned with your financial objectives. This can be crucial if you're concentrating on fortifying your retirement nest egg in these decisive years.

Another factor to ponder is the scale of time. How long do you plan to stay in your next home? Traditionally, buying a home is advantageous if you're planning on living in it for several years, as this allows time for the property to appreciate in value, hopefully surpassing the costs involved in purchasing and selling the home. If you envision a future that may involve downsizing, relocating, or even extensive travel, renting could provide the flexibility that ownership can't match.

Consider, too, the comfort of predictability. A fixed-rate mortgage offers consistent monthly payments until your home is paid off, barring changes in property taxes or homeowner's insurance. Rent, however, is subject to inflation and can increase with time, subject to the terms of your lease and local laws. Determine which scenario best aligns with your need for foreseeable expenses.

Maintenance is another cornerstone in this debate. As a homeowner, you'll be solely responsible for all the upkeep and repairs

– a reality that can be both costly and time-consuming. Renters are typically relieved of most of these responsibilities, with landlords shouldering the duties and expenses of property maintenance. Assess your willingness and ability to handle home repairs, both from a financial and a physical standpoint.

Additionally, the concept of home should resonate with personal freedom and choice. As a homeowner, you have the liberty to alter your dwelling as you see fit. Want to knock down a wall, change the flooring, or plant a garden? You're free to create the home you've always wanted. Renting, on the other hand, typically limits these freedoms, but it does so without burdening you with the responsibilities of ownership.

Let's not overlook the important aspect of mobility. Buying a home can anchor you to a specific location, with the average time to break even on a home purchase hovering around five years, depending on the market. This may not complement one's future plans if they involve relocation for leisure, closer proximity to family, or even senior living arrangements. Renting maintains your ability to move with greater ease and less financial impact.

Delving into the emotional tapestry, owning a home can imbue a sense of belonging and community that may be paramount for many. It's not merely a financial transaction; it's where life unfolds, where memories are made, and where a sense of permanence is established. However, renting can cultivate a similar sense of home without the binding commitment of ownership.

For those who have grappled with debt or budgeting challenges in the past, the predictability of renting may also offer a sense of financial security. The costs associated with renting are generally steady and more predictable in the short term, which can be comforting for those who have worked hard to achieve financial stability and do not want to risk unexpected homeownership costs.

Contemplate the current real estate market conditions as well. In a seller's market with high property prices, you might find yourself wrestling with bidding wars and overpriced inventory. Renting might allow you to wait out the frenzy until the market cools down and more favorable buying conditions emerge. However, in a buyer's market, you might find opportunities to purchase a home at a lower cost and with better terms.

Tax considerations are also critical at this juncture of your life. The potential for mortgage interest and property tax deductions can sway the scales in favor of buying from a tax perspective. However, these benefits are not as substantial as they once were for many, due to changes in tax laws and depending on personal situations. Analyze your specific financial picture and tax implications with the guidance of a tax professional before proceeding.

Furthermore, simplicity might be what you are yearning for in these golden years. Renting can offer a straightforward lifestyle without the complexities of property taxes, homeowners association fees, and unexpected repairs. Especially as you prioritize ease and leisure in later life, the simplicity of renting might be the appealing choice.

A critical step in this journey is to align your housing decision with your long-term financial and life goals. If travel, flexibility, and minimal responsibility are pillars of your retirement vision, renting might underpin these aspirations beautifully. If stability, rootedness, and long-term financial planning are more your rhythm, buying could be the key to your future harmony.

In conclusion, there is no universally right answer when deciding to buy or rent in later life. Your financial landscape, personal goals, lifestyle preferences, and the current economic climate all play instrumental roles in this decision. What remains constant is your ability to choose – to scribe your narrative with the decisions that best suit you at this moment in life. It's not about the age on your driver's license, but the dreams in your heart and the reality of your financial situation. In the end, the place you call home should be the setting for your greatest contentment, regardless of whether you hold its deed or lease.

As we cinematically pan across the horizon, remember that your home – be it rented or owned – is where your life's stories unfold. Make it a sanctuary that reflects your desires, suits your financial comfort zone, and inspires peace and happiness. The walls that surround you should empower your later life journey, not constrict it. Choose wisely, and may your home be the cornerstone of a vibrant, financially secure future.

Managing Mortgages and Equity

Home ownership can be a cornerstone of financial stability and a quintessential part of the American Dream. As you navigate this pathway, understanding how to manage mortgages and home equity becomes crucial, particularly when you're fortifying your finances later in life.

Mortgages are not just loans; they're stepping stones towards building equity. Every mortgage payment made is a stride towards increasing your stake in your property. And with that equity comes a powerful financial tool you can leverage to meet various goals, from consolidating debt to funding a retirement account or even financing a child's education.

First and foremost, it's vital to select the right mortgage. Find an option that suits your financial situation now and in the future. While a 30-year mortgage may offer lower monthly payments, a 15-year term could save you a considerable amount in interest over the life of the loan. Be mindful of interest rates and the impact they have over time.

Remember, what appears small in percentage points can translate into tens of thousands of dollars.

Once you secure a mortgage, focus on payment management. If you can, consider bi-weekly payments instead of monthly. This strategy can shave years off your mortgage term and save a remarkable amount in interest, as you'll make one extra payment each year. And always, before implementing this or any strategy, ensure it aligns with your budget and other financial commitments.

What about refinancing? With changing interest rates, refinancing your mortgage could lower your monthly payments and total interest cost. It's not a decision to be taken lightly, though. Refinancing entails costs and fees, and it's important to do a breakeven analysis to understand if and when you'll recoup those costs through your savings on interest.

Now, let's talk home equity. It's the difference between the value of your home and what you owe on your mortgage. This equity is an asset, one that increases as your mortgage balance decreases and as your home's value appreciates. To access it, you might consider a home equity loan or a home equity line of credit (HELOC). Both provide liquidity but use your home as collateral, which requires careful contemplation.

Home equity loans are akin to second mortgages, doling out a lump sum that's repaid over a set term. Fixed interest rates make these loans predictable, but remember, taking out a loan against your home's equity reduces the equity you have built.

Similarly, HELOCs offer flexibility with a line of credit you draw on as needed. The variable interest rate that often comes with HELOCs can be a double-edged sword – attractive when rates are low, but potentially costly if rates rise.

Regardless of the approach you take to access home equity, be prudent. While it can fund important endeavors, using it for non-essential purchases can imperil your financial security. Your home is both an investment and a sanctuary; using its value should always be a measured decision.

Additionally, always be aware of property taxes and insurance. They can alter your mortgage payments if you have an escrow account, and a significant change in property value or tax rates can impact your financial planning. Monitoring these expenses and adjusting your escrow contributions can prevent unwelcome surprises.

Another critical aspect of mortgage management is preparation for economic downturns. If challenges arise, know that options like loan modification, forbearance, or even federally backed relief programs may be available to prevent foreclosure.

For those with substantial equity in their homes, reverse mortgages may present an option later in life, typically after reaching 62 years of age. This allows homeowners to convert part of their equity into cash without selling the home. However, navigate this area with caution and thorough research, as reverse mortgages can have long-term implications for your finances and estate planning.

As you pursue managing mortgages and home equity, always maintain balance. It's important to invest in your home, but not at the expense of other critical financial goals, like saving for retirement. Diversification is just as important in personal finance as it is in investments.

To conclude, remember that managing your mortgage and home equity effectively requires a comprehensive understanding of the financial landscape, a clear-eyed view of your long-term goals, and a commitment to making informed decisions. Whether you're nearing retirement or planning for the years ahead, your home's value can be a significant asset. Use it wisely, and it will serve as a powerful component of your financial health and legacy.

As you close this chapter, take a moment to reflect on how you can apply these insights to enhance your financial well-being. In the pursuit of security and comfort in later years, a well-managed home can be both a dependable shelter and a financial bulwark.

CHAPTER 7: NAVIGATING THE INSURANCE MAZE

As we journey further into mastering our financial landscape, it's essential to chart a path through the often perplexing world of insurance. Insurance isn't merely a safety net—it's a critical component for peace of mind and fiscal security, especially after hitting the milestone age of 40. Whether it's parsing the intricacies of health insurance policies post-employment benefits or understanding the nuances of life insurance and long-term care options, the goal is to become well-versed in the policies that will best serve your unique needs. Decisions made about these insurance vehicles affect not just your present financial standing, but also the legacy you wish to build. With a focus on clarity and strategic selection, this chapter empowers you to make informed insurance choices that resonate with the life you envision for yourself and your loved ones. It's about harnessing knowledge to turn the insurance maze into a mapped-out journey, guiding you toward a future where you can stand confident in your financial shield against life's unforeseeable events.

Health Insurance Options After 40

As you've navigated through the essentials of budgeting, saving strategies, and investing, let's delve into a critical element of your financial health: insurance. Specifically, health insurance. Approaching or residing in the post-40 club often triggers a heightened awareness of health and wellness. It's not about pessimism; it's about prudence.

Health insurance after 40 becomes increasingly important – and sometimes, more complex.

Turning 40 can serve as an important milestone for reevaluating your health insurance needs. Perhaps you've been riding the wave of a workplace group plan, but it's imperative to understand that personal health insurance needs tend to evolve with age. The time is ripe to explore the options available to you, each with its benefits and considerations.

For starters, employer-sponsored health plans are a staple for many. They often provide comprehensive coverage at a subsidized cost due to the employer's financial contribution. However, staying informed about changes in coverage, network, and costs as you age is vital. An annual review is wise to ensure the plan still meets your changing health needs.

If you're self-employed or do not have access to an employer-sponsored plan, individual health insurance plans are your go-to. The marketplace under the Affordable Care Act offers various plans with differing levels of coverage and premiums. It's key to compare the cost versus benefits, taking into account not just the monthly premium but also deductibles, co-pays, and out-of-pocket maximums.

Then there's the Health Savings Account (HSA) eligible high-deductible health plans (HDHP). They're powerful tools if you're generally healthy and looking to save for future health expenses on a tax-advantaged basis. With an HSA, you can roll over funds year to year, investing them for potential growth.

Once you reach age 50, it's smart to start getting familiar with the ins and outs of Medicare. Original Medicare, including Part A and B, covers hospital and medical costs, respectively, but it's not comprehensive. You'll need to decide whether to add Part D for prescription drugs and possibly Medigap for supplemental coverage, or opt for a Medicare Advantage plan, which is like an all-in-one alternative.

Don't skip considering Long-Term Care insurance; the likelihood of needing some form of long-term care increases as you age. This type of insurance can help manage the costs associated with long-term care services, which are typically not covered by standard health insurance or Medicare.

What about those with pre-existing conditions? Thanks to healthcare reforms, being denied coverage has become a relic of the past. While this is a relief, it's important to carefully weigh the costs of plans that accommodate pre-existing conditions, as they may be pricier.

Beyond the federal programs, individual states might offer health benefit programs catering to middle-aged individuals. Researching state-sponsored programs can uncover additional options or supplements to your primary coverage that are more tailored to your phase of life.

Don't overlook the importance of preventative care. Many insurance plans offer preventative services at little or no cost. Engaging in regular health maintenance can save on future costs and provide the roadmap to a healthier lifestyle.

Understand that health insurance isn't merely a standalone topic—it's intricately tied to your overall financial strategy. The right coverage can protect your finances from unexpected medical costs that could otherwise derail your retirement savings or other financial goals.

Remember, open enrollment periods are key windows during which you can make changes to your coverage. Missing these can result in staying locked into a less-than-ideal plan for another year or paying penalties. Keep a calendar reminder for these crucial dates.

It's also important to consider the perks and wellness programs that may come with different health plans. Some offer gym memberships, nutritional consultations, or health monitoring programs. These additions, while seemingly minor, can contribute to long-term wellness and potentially lower health expenses over time.

Finally, while researching and selecting health insurance can be a dense and, at times, a confusing process, it doesn't have to be a solitary one. Utilize resources like state health insurance assistance programs, financial advisors, or even consultations with insurance providers to gain clarity.

Predicaments aside, seeing the bigger picture can be empowering. Your post-40 years are an opportunity to prioritize your well-being, with health insurance being a significant part of that puzzle. A forward-thinking approach to medical coverage is more than just planning—it's ensuring that your later chapters are lived with peace of mind and security. Embrace it with the diligence and care it—and you—deserve.

Life Insurance and Long-Term Care Policies

As you steer through the complexities of financial planning after 40, it's crucial to shine a light on two significant aspects of your security blanket: life insurance and long-term care policies. These instruments are not just policies but are pillars that can uphold your family's financial well-being and help preserve your hard-earned assets in the event of life's unpredictable turns.

Life insurance, in essence, is about risk management. It's a safety net, offering peace of mind that your loved ones will be financially protected if you're no longer there to provide for them. While the thought may seem somber, it's a necessary consideration. Begin by evaluating your unique situation; do you have dependents who rely on your income? Are there debts or a mortgage that need to be covered?

Answering these questions will help determine the amount and type of coverage that best suits your needs.

Term life insurance is often a cost-effective choice for those who need coverage for a specific period, say until your children are financially independent, or your mortgage is paid off. On the other hand, permanent life insurance, such as whole life or universal life, provides lifelong coverage and can contribute to your financial strategy through cash value accumulation, with the potential to borrow against it if the need arises.

On the other side of the coin lie long-term care policies. The prospect of requiring long-term care is something many overlook, but it's a stark reality for a significant portion of the elderly population. These policies can cover services that aren't typically provided by health insurance, Medicare, or Medicaid, such as assistance with daily activities and nursing home care.

Securing a long-term care policy earlier in life can often lock in lower premiums since age and health are prime factors in determining cost. Wait until you're older or after a major health diagnosis, and you might find premiums unaffordable or coverage unattainable.

Understanding the variety of long-term care policies is crucial. There are traditional policies that strictly cover long-term care, and hybrid policies that combine life insurance with long-term care benefits. The right choice depends on your financial situation, health, and personal preferences.

It's also important to delve into the benefits each policy provides. For instance, consider the daily benefit amount, the length of time the policy will pay out, and any waiting periods before the benefits kick in. Additionally, explore any inflation protection offered, which can be vital given the rising cost of care.

When evaluating life insurance and long-term care policies, it's not only about what you buy, but also from whom you buy it. Look for reputable insurers with strong financial stability and history of fair claims processing. This due diligence is essential in ensuring that your policy is there for you when you need it the most.

Moreover, it's imperative to review these policies periodically. Life's changes might necessitate adjustments to your coverage. A new marriage, divorce, birth of a child, home purchase, or change in business ownership are all significant events that should trigger a policy review.

The cost of life insurance and long-term care coverage can feel overwhelming, but it's a mistake to forgo these policies entirely due to expense. More often than not, there are options to fit various budgets; you just need to explore them.

Consult with financial experts who specialize in insurance to help you navigate these decisions. They can provide invaluable insights into which policies match your needs and how they integrate with your overall financial plan. Your goal here isn't just to buy a policy, but to make an informed investment in your and your family's future.

Lastly, remember that life insurance and long-term care are about more than just numbers and premiums; they're about values and priorities. By securing the right coverage, you're not only safeguarding your assets but also honoring the responsibilities you have to those you love. Making these decisions with clarity and confidence will grant you and your loved ones the peace of mind that can't be quantified.

Therefore, as you continue to tread through the insurance maze, give life insurance and long-term care the attention they deserve. They're vital components of a comprehensive financial plan and serve as a testament to your foresight and dedication to your family's well-being. Unlike other forms of insurance, these policies assure that whether life takes you on a journey long and full or cuts it unfairly short, your financial plans remain intact, and your legacy lives on.

As you move to the next chapters, where we will touch on retirement planning and estate considerations, keep in mind that life insurance and long-term care policies are closely intertwined within these topics. Together, they form a trinity of financial security that fortifies your future and ensures your life's work transcends your lifetime.

CHAPTER 8: RETIREMENT PLANNING FOR LATE STARTERS

It's never too late to embark on the journey to a financially secure retirement, and for those who've gotten a late start, it's crucial to navigate the path with strategic precision. Tailoring a retirement plan in the latter stage of one's career means understanding both the challenges and the unique opportunities that come with a condensed time frame. We delve into methods for accurately projecting retirement needs while maximizing every opportunity for growth, such as catch-up contributions that can supercharge your savings. Equally important are the tax considerations that can significantly impact your nest egg, presenting both hurdles and gateways to stretch your dollars further. In this chapter, embracing a proactive stance on retirement preparation will pave the way for achieving peace of mind and the financial freedom to enjoy your golden years with confidence and grace. Harnessing the power of informed decision-making and strategic financial maneuvers, you can craft a retirement that's as robust and secure as any lifelong planner's.

Estimating Retirement Needs and Costs

When it comes to retirement planning, understanding the future you're aiming for is as important as knowing where you stand today. Estimating your retirement needs is a complex, but essential step in the journey towards a comfortable retirement, especially if you're getting a later start. It's about more than picking a number out of thin air; it's about envisioning the lifestyle you desire and aligning it with realistic financial targets.

To begin, calculate your current expenses. Monitor your bank statements, receipts, and bills to get an accurate sense of your monthly expenses. Don't forget to include sporadic costs like car maintenance or holiday spending. This baseline is crucial as it offers a snapshot of your current cost of living, which, adjusted for inflation and altered circumstances, can provide a rough estimate of your retirement needs.

It's vital to acknowledge changes in retirement. You might have your mortgage paid off by then, but your healthcare costs could potentially rise. You also might spend less on commuting but more on hobbies or travel. These shifts in spending patterns need to be carefully considered when estimating retirement costs.

One method to estimate retirement expenses is the 'replacement rate' strategy. The idea here is that you will need 70-80% of your pre-retirement income to maintain your lifestyle once you retire. This rule of thumb accounts for the decrease in taxes, work-related expenses, and savings contributions. But don't just rely on generic guidelines; tailor your estimate to your aspirations and health predictions.

Account for inflation, which can erode your purchasing power over time. Historically, inflation has averaged around 3% per year, but this can fluctuate. Use an online retirement calculator to factor inflation into your estimates, ensuring your retirement savings target maintains its value over time.

Next, take longevity into account. With advances in healthcare, many people live well into their 90s. Plan for a long life to avoid outliving your assets. This may mean planning for a retirement that could last as long as your working life did.

Another consideration is healthcare expenses. As you age, these costs often increase, and they can be significant. Examine options for

Medicare and supplemental insurance, and get a sense of what out-of-pocket expenses might look like. Long-term care insurance might also be worth considering, as long-term care is often not covered by standard health insurance.

Social Security benefits can reduce your savings burden. Create an account on the Social Security Administration's website to get an estimate of your projected benefits. However, be cautious with these numbers. It's prudent to think of Social Security as a supplement rather than a primary source of income.

Don't forget to consider the impact of taxes on your retirement savings. Withdrawals from traditional retirement accounts, like IRAs and 401(k)s, are taxed at ordinary income rates. Planning for these taxes in advance can prevent unpleasant surprises and protect your net income in retirement.

If you have multiple sources of potential retirement income, such as a part-time job, rental income, or annuities, include these in your calculations. These can provide additional buffers to your savings and even allow for a more luxurious retirement lifestyle.

Once you have a clearer picture of what you might need, compare it against your current trajectory. Are your savings and investment plans on track to meet these needs? If there's a gap, you'll need to consider how to close it – whether through higher contributions, adjusting your investment strategy, or possibly rethinking your desired retirement lifestyle.

Remember to review and adjust your estimates regularly. As you progress through life, your desired lifestyle, health status, and economic circumstances can change. Keep refining your retirement plan to ensure it remains aligned with your evolving needs and goals.

For those who've started late, it's tempting to feel overwhelmed by the magnitude of what needs to be saved. But remember, with each step you're forging a path to a more secure future. Even modest savings can grow over time, thanks to the power of compounding interest. The key is to start now and keep building consistently.

Reaching your late-start retirement goals requires discipline, perseverance, and positive action. Each choice you make, from cutting needless expenses to boosting your savings rate, can create a ripple of financial improvement. Think of every dollar saved as another brick in the foundation of your future security.

And finally, don't hesitate to seek professional advice. A financial advisor can be a valuable ally in helping you navigate the complexities of retirement planning. They can offer personalized strategies to maximize your savings and investments, keeping you on course towards achieving a fulfilling and well-deserved retirement.

Catch-Up Contributions and Tax Considerations

Beginning to save for retirement later in life can feel daunting, but it's important to recognize that it's never too late to make significant progress. One often overlooked strategy for late starters is maximizing catch-up contributions. As you embark on bolstering your retirement savings, understanding and utilizing catch-up contributions can be a pivotal piece of your financial plan.

Catch-up contributions are extra amounts that individuals over a certain age can add to their retirement savings accounts. If you've crossed the age of 50, the IRS allows you to contribute additional funds over the standard limit to your 401(k), IRA, or other retirement accounts. These contributions not only aid in growing your nest egg but also have potential tax benefits that can effectively reduce your taxable income.

In the complex world of retirement savings, tax implications play a critical role. When considering retirement planning, it's essential to understand how your contributions affect your taxes both today and in the future. Traditional retirement accounts like 401(k)s and traditional IRAs offer tax-deferred growth, meaning you won't pay taxes on the money you contribute until you withdraw it in retirement.

Catch-up contributions increase the amount you can save tax-deferred, effectively lowering your current taxable income. This can be particularly beneficial if you're in a higher income bracket, as the reduction in taxable income could potentially drop you into a lower tax bracket, saving you money on your tax bill.

On the other hand, contributions to Roth accounts are made with after-tax dollars. However, the benefit of a Roth account, be it a Roth IRA or Roth 401(k), is that the withdrawals in retirement are tax-free, assuming certain conditions are met. This can be a strategic advantage if you anticipate being in a higher tax bracket in retirement or if tax rates rise across the board.

It's pivotal to remember that tax laws are complex and subject to change. Keeping abreast of current regulations and how they impact your retirement planning is crucial. It's always advisable to consult with a tax professional who can provide personalized advice based on your specific financial situation.

Not only do catch-up contributions offer tax benefits, but they also can have a compounding effect on your retirement savings. The more you put into your accounts now, the more potential growth you can accrue over time. This is one of the primary reasons to take advantage of catch-up contributions as soon as you're eligible.

Another key tax consideration is the timing of your contributions. If you expect your income to be higher in a particular year, you might want to increase that year's contributions to offset the tax burden. Conversely, if you expect a lower income year, it may be wiser to allocate more funds to Roth contributions, paying taxes now while you're in a lower bracket.

Withdrawal rules are also a critical aspect of retirement planning, particularly with traditional retirement accounts. Required Minimum Distributions (RMDs) are amounts that the federal government requires you to withdraw annually from certain types of retirement accounts starting at age 72. These amounts are based on your account balance and life expectancy, and not taking RMDs can result in hefty penalties.

Planning for RMDs is important as they can have significant tax implications, especially if you have large balances in your tax-deferred accounts. It's crucial to include RMDs in your retirement income strategy to ensure you're not suddenly bumped into a higher tax bracket upon taking these mandatory distributions.

In some circumstances, late starters may also have the opportunity to make deductible IRA contributions that can reduce their taxable income. If you or your spouse aren't covered by a retirement plan at work, you can deduct the full amount of your IRA contribution, regardless of income. This is another avenue where tax savings can be substantial.

Furthermore, the Saver's Credit is a tax credit available to eligible taxpayers who make contributions to their retirement accounts. It's designed to encourage low and middle-income individuals to save for retirement. Depending on your adjusted gross income and your tax filing status, you could claim a portion of your retirement contributions as a tax credit, directly reducing your tax bill.

As you navigate retirement planning at a later stage, it's fundamental to weave catch-up contributions and tax considerations into your strategy. This approach not only maximizes your saving capability but also empowers you to make informed decisions that can lead to a more secure and comfortable retirement.

Endowed with this knowledge, take a proactive stance in managing your retirement funds. Explore every avenue to expand your contributions and be tactful with your tax planning. Harness the benefits of catch-up contributions to not only close the gap in your retirement savings but to bolster your future financial independence.

Lastly, maintain a resilient mindset as you fortify your financial foundation. Starting later does not preclude success; it merely means you have to navigate the landscape with a sharper focus and an unwavering commitment. Remember, with each step forward, you're not just planning for retirement, but you're also crafting a legacy of financial security and peace of mind for yourself and your loved ones.

CHAPTER 9: ESTATE PLANNING AND WILLS

Embarking on estate planning may seem daunting, yet it's a fundamental cornerstone for safeguarding your legacy and ensuring your wishes are fulfilled. Within Chapter 9, we delve into the intricacies of crafting a comprehensive will and the establishment of trusts, tools that are quintessential in delineating the destiny of your assets posthumously. You'll learn that a will is more than a document—it's a declaration of your intentions, an assurance that your hard-earned assets are allocated according to your desires. We'll guide you through the critical components of what constitutes a legally binding will, the nuanced differences between various types of trusts and their purposes, and how they can provide both protection for your beneficiaries and potential tax benefits. Further, this chapter underscores the importance of creating health care directives and setting up power of attorney—preparations that speak for you when you're unable to vocalize your healthcare preferences and decisions. Empowering you with the knowledge to navigate these waters, this chapter aims to imbue you with the confidence to forge an estate plan that embodies your values and secures peace of mind for you and your loved ones.

Establishing a Will and Trusts

Talking about the future, especially our absence in it, might feel uncomfortable and often overlooked, but planning ahead is a key step in securing your legacy and ensuring your assets are managed according to your wishes. Establishing a will and setting up trusts are two cornerstones in robust estate planning. Let's delve into these crucial components to help lay the groundwork for a stable future for those we care about.

A will, often referred to as a last will and testament, is a legally binding document that articulates how you'd like your assets and personal matters handled after you pass away. Without a will, state laws dictate who receives your assets, which may not align with your personal wishes. Thus, crafting a will can provide you with peace of mind, knowing that you're in control of who benefits from your life's work.

The process of creating a will starts with taking inventory of your assets, which include not just your finances and real estate, but also personal items that might hold sentimental value to your loved ones. This inventory is a revealing exercise, sometimes bringing to light the full scope of what you'll be leaving behind.

When you're ready to write your will, it's often advisable to consult with a legal professional, especially if your estate involves substantial assets or complicated family dynamics. However, if your situation is straightforward, there are reputable online services that guide you through creating a legally sound document for your state. Whichever route you choose, ensure your will is not only written but also properly signed, witnessed, and notarized, as per your state's requirements.

Now, while a will is fundamental, there are certain limitations. It becomes public record once it's filed for probate, it doesn't avoid probate court, and can sometimes be a lengthy process. This is where trusts can offer a supplemental solution. A trust is a fiduciary arrangement that allows a third party, or trustee, to hold assets on behalf of a beneficiary or beneficiaries.

There are various types of trusts to consider. A revocable living trust, for example, offers flexibility during your lifetime, allowing you to alter or void the arrangement as you see fit. You can move assets in and out of the trust while you're alive, and then, upon your death, these assets can be transferred to your beneficiaries without the need for probate court, keeping your estate matters private and often resulting in quicker distribution.

Irrevocable trusts, contrarily, cannot be changed once they're established. They can be beneficial for tax considerations and protecting assets from legal judgements. They're also not considered your personal property once they've been set up, so the assets in an irrevocable trust typically aren't subject to estate taxes.

When you're setting up a trust, it's imperative to choose your trustee wisely. This individual or institution will manage the trust's assets and carry out your wishes, so selecting someone who is trustworthy, competent, and has an understanding of your values is paramount.

Setting up trusts can be complex, and navigating the legal jargon and tax implications can be daunting. It's usually best to engage an estate planning attorney to tailor your trust in such a way that it aligns with your specific needs and estate planning goals. This professional can also help you understand the nuances between different types of trusts and how they can serve your estate most effectively.

Moreover, trusts aren't exclusive to the ultra-wealthy. They're practical tools for many different scenarios, such as managing assets for minor children or adults who might not be capable of overseeing an inheritance. This is a crucial consideration for anyone wanting to provide for loved ones who need future assistance.

An often overlooked aspect of establishing trusts is conveying your intentions to your beneficiaries and trustees. This clarity eases future transitions and helps avoid misunderstands or conflicts. It's a good idea to have open conversations with those who will be involved in your estate to ensure they understand your wishes and the reasons behind them.

Beneficiary designations are another important element in any estate plan. Assets like insurance policies and retirement accounts typically bypass the will and go directly to the named beneficiaries. Therefore, they must be aligned with your overall estate plan, and should be updated after life changing events such as marriage, divorce, or the birth of a child.

Remember, estate planning, including wills and trusts, are not set-and-forget actions. You should review and possibly update your estate plan regularly, at least every few years or after significant life changes. Laws also change, so it's important that your documents remain current and legally robust. Estate planning ensures that when the time comes, your legacy is preserved and your wishes are fulfilled, offering you tranquility now and sparing your loved ones unnecessary stress later.

While deliberating your estate plan might evoke a mix of emotions, remember that it's a profound act of responsibility and love towards your family and dependents. It's an enduring statement of your life's values and your commitment to their well-being, long after you're gone.

Embarking on this journey of establishing a will and trusts may initially feel daunting, but envision it as constructing a bridge that will safely carry your loved ones into the future. Your thoughtful planning today lays down the planks for that bridge, plank by plank, ensuring a smooth and secure passage.

As you continue to read through this book and absorb the knowledge within these pages, let's carry forward the spirit of empowerment and foresight. With thoughtful planning, focused action, and a guided hand, you can confidently navigate the path toward a stable and prosperous future for yourself and those dear to you.

Health Care Directives and Power of Attorney

As we journey through the prime of our lives, becoming adept at charting a course through the seas of estate planning is not just prudent—it's imperative. Health Care Directives and Power of Attorney (POA) are pivotal elements in the safeguarding of your health and financial decisions. These legal instruments ensure that your wishes are honored should you become unable to vocalize them due to health considerations.

Let's wade into the specifics of a Health Care Directive, often called a "living will." This document outlines your preferences for medical treatment in a variety of scenarios where you may not be able to make decisions for yourself. It's a declaration of your healthcare desires, granting peace of mind not only to you, but also to your loved ones and medical professionals.

It's important to note that a living will is different from a "do not resuscitate" order, which is more restrictive and specific. Instead, a Health Care Directive can cover a range of interventions—from life-prolonging treatments to palliative care preferences—enabling you to maintain control over your medical care.

Complementing Health Care Directives is the Durable Power of Attorney for Health Care, also known as a health care proxy. Whereas the directive lays out your medical wishes, this POA appoints a trusted individual to make healthcare decisions on your behalf if you're incapacitated. This person, your proxy, steps into your shoes, armed with the intimate knowledge of your values and wishes, to guide decision-makers toward choices you would have made yourself.

Moving to the fiscal side, a Financial Power of Attorney assigns a person or organization the authority to handle your financial affairs. This can include paying your bills, managing your investments, or even selling property. Vigilance in selecting someone for this role can't be understated, as they will be your financial alter-ego, acting in your best interests.

You may be wondering: When does a Power of Attorney become effective? There are two main types: a "springing" POA, which only activates under conditions specified in the document—typically a medical determination of incapacity—and a "durable" POA, which is effective immediately upon signing and remains in effect if you become incapacitated.

Ensuring fundamental conversations about these matters happen before drafting these documents is essential. Who you appoint under a POA holds significant gravity and discussing your philosophy of life, ideas about extended medical care, and financial management with your chosen proxies solidifies your expectations.

It's also crucial to re-evaluate these documents periodically, especially after major life events: marriage, divorce, the birth of new family members, or the loss of a designated representative. Life's undulating nature means what was pertinent yesterday may not hold the same weight today.

Documentation alone doesn't complete the process, though. You have to communicate these decisions clearly to both your healthcare providers and family members, ensuring there are no surprises or uncertainties in a time of crisis. Transparency breeds readiness and eases the emotional burden on your family during tough times.

Moreover, laws regarding Health Care Directives and POAs can vary by state, so it is crucial to ensure your documents meet your state's legal requirements. This is where employing the expertise of a skilled estate planning attorney becomes invaluable—their guidance can navigate the variegated state-specific requirements and guarantee that your documents hold up when they're needed most.

You may feel a sense of apprehension about confronting less-than-rosy subjects such as potential incapacity or end-of-life care, but preparation in this realm is as much a part of loving stewardship over your life as making wise financial investments. It's an assertion that you're charting your destiny, steering firmly even amidst unforeseen storms.

If you've yet to address Health Care Directives and POAs in your estate plan, consider this as a call to action. Take a step towards drafting these key documents. It's never too early to protect your autonomy and provide clarity for your loved ones. It's an action that echoes responsibility, foresight, and respect for life's uncertain tide.

Health Care Directives and Powers of Attorney may involve filling out standardized forms, yet each person's situation is nuanced. This means personalized advice from trained professionals is not just helpful—it's a necessity for a document fully tuned to your life's unique symphony.

As you carry forth in your financial journey, tie in the loose ends with a concise and comprehensive estate plan that includes Health Care Directives and Powers of Attorney. It's a step beyond the financial—it's an embrace of your life's narrative, affirming that your story will be honored and your voice heard through whatever may come.

CHAPTER 10: CREATING PASSIVE INCOME STREAMS

As we step closer towards a future of financial independence, constructing a fortress of passive income becomes more than a luxury—it transforms into an essential pillar of a well-rounded financial strategy. By exploring the avenues of earning where you're not actively trading your time for money, you're granting yourself the opportunity to diversify your income and potentially buffer against life's uncertainties. Whether it's rental property income, dividends from a well-curated stock portfolio, or a venture into the realm of royalties from creative work, each stream acts like a tributary, collectively feeding into the mighty river of financial security. Now, while the groundwork for these income streams may require some initial effort or investment, mastering the balance of risk and reward can pave the path to prosperity. And with some nurturing and strategic planning, these passive sources can flourish, offering you the freedom to pursue your passions or simply enjoy the peace that comes with a stable and secure late-life financial landscape.

Identifying Opportunities for Passive Income

As we navigate the path to financial resilience, the allure of passive income cannot be overstated. Passive income, the holy grail for many, is earnings derived from a source in which the investor is not actively involved. Let's embark on a journey to uncover the often-unseen opportunities to create passive income streams that fit harmoniously into your life's tapestry.

The first step is to recognize that passive income opportunities are all around us. They require a discerning eye and a willingness to think creatively. Venturing into the realm of real estate, for example, can be a lucrative start. Rental properties offer an enduring source of passive income for those prepared to manage tenants and upkeep. Real estate investment trusts (REITs) provide a more hands-off approach, allowing one to reap the benefits of the real estate market without directly managing properties.

Dividend stocks are another solid pillar when building passive income. They represent a share of profits from companies paid out regularly to shareholders. By investing in stable companies with a history of dividend payments, you can create a stream of income that works for you while you sleep.

Peer-to-peer lending platforms present a modern avenue for passive income. These platforms allow you to lend money to individuals or small businesses online, gaining income through interest payments. It's essential, however, to be aware of the default risks associated with lending.

Another consideration is the creation of digital assets. In the age of information, content is king. Writing an e-book, creating an online course, or developing a mobile application can generate ongoing income after the initial effort of creation. The digital world offers myriad opportunities for those who can navigate its terrain effectively.

For the artistically inclined, licensing your work or producing stock photography can yield a steady stream of royalties. As businesses and creators are continuously in search of fresh content, your creative output can become a gift that keeps on giving.

Bond ladders, a strategy of purchasing multiple bonds with different maturity dates, is yet another method for generating passive income. This approach can provide regular interest payments as bonds mature over time, and reduce interest rate risk by diversifying maturities.

Exploring affiliate marketing can also be rewarding. By promoting products or services on a blog, social media, or a website, you can earn commissions for customer referrals. A robust online presence and an engaged audience are crucial for success in this field.

For those accustomed to the traditional workforce, starting a side business could shift the balance from active to passive income over time. Whether it's a laundromat, vending machines, or an automated online business, the initial groundwork can blossom into a self-sustaining source of income.

Additionally, owning a small business presents an opportunity to eventually step back and let the business operate independently, while still enjoying the profits. The key is to build a business that can thrive under the management of others, making it a passive rather than active investment.

One should not forget the power of automation in the quest for passive income. Investing in funds that track an index, known as index funds, allows one's investments to grow with the market trend, requiring minimal intervention and fees.

Among these opportunities, there lies the allure of exclusivity. Membership sites and subscription services offer another avenue to recurring income. By providing continuous value, patrons will remain, contributing regularly to your income stream.

Furthermore, investing in startups or small businesses can be a potent way to generate passive income. One can either become a silent partner or use a platform for crowdfunding investments to find opportunities that align with your interests and financial goals.

An essential aspect of identifying passive income opportunities is aligning them with your financial objectives and lifestyle preferences.

You must always perform thorough due diligence and seek out investments that not only promise a return but resonate with your values and long-term goals.

In conclusion, the landscape for passive income generation is vast and varied. It requires savvy, patience, and an appetite for strategic planning. The objective is to build a diverse portfolio of passive income streams that support your financial ambitions, providing you with the financial security and freedom to enjoy life on your terms. Each opportunity has its unique merits and challenges, but the key is to start somewhere, learn as you go, and progressively build your passive income repertoire.

Risks and Rewards of Different Passive Avenues

Embarking on the journey of creating passive income is akin to cultivating a garden; it takes time, effort, and patience to see the fruits of labor. Many avenues exist to generate passive income, each with its own set of risks and potential rewards. It's imperative to navigate these paths thoughtfully, especially when one strives for financial security later in life.

One of the most traditional paths to passive income is through dividend-paying stocks. By investing in established companies with a track record of distributing profits to shareholders, one can potentially enjoy a stream of passive income. However, the stock market is volatile, and there's always the risk of dividend cuts or, worse, company bankruptcy.

Another avenue is real estate. Rental properties can provide a steady cash flow and property values may appreciate over time. Nevertheless, the responsibilities of being a landlord often merge with challenges like vacancies, maintenance issues, and the potential for problematic tenants. Additionally, real estate markets can fluctuate, impacting rental yields and property values.

Bonds, with their fixed-interest payments, are often regarded as a safer option. They can provide a reliable income, but the trade-off for this security is typically lower returns. There's also the risk that inflation will outpace the interest earned, diminishing your purchasing power.

Peer-to-peer lending platforms have emerged as a way to generate income by lending money directly to individuals or small businesses. While these can offer attractive returns, they come with the risk of default. Unlike banks, individuals don't have the same resources to vet borrowers or recoup losses.

Then there's the potential of creating an online business that can generate passive income through sales of products or advertising revenue. Initial efforts might be substantial in creating content or products, but once the business gains traction, it could sustainably generate income. Keep in mind, the digital world is competitive, and maintaining an online business requires constant updates and marketing strategies.

Investing in a business as a silent partner is another way to earn passive income. It allows one to benefit from profits without daily involvement. The risk, however, lies in the business's performance, which is out of one's direct control. Thorough due diligence is essential before committing to such an investment.

Royalties from intellectual property, such as books, music, or patents, can also provide a passive income source. While the creation of such works can be incredibly rewarding, there is no guarantee of success, and upfront costs may be significant without the promise of return.

High-yield savings accounts and certificates of deposit (CDs) offer minimal risk but also lower returns. The advantage is the predictability and security of income, making them suitable for those who prefer stability over higher, riskier gains.

Annuities are insurance products that can provide a steady income stream in retirement. However, they can be complex financial products with high fees, and once committed, your funds may be locked in or have potentially expensive withdrawal fees. Understanding the terms thoroughly is crucial before purchasing an annuity.

Crowdfunded investments have opened up new passive income opportunities, from real estate projects to innovative startups. These platforms can lead to diversification and potentially significant returns but come with the lack of liquidity and the chance that projects don't go as planned.

For the artistically inclined, selling artwork or photographs on platforms designed for passive revenue can be appealing. However, the market is crowded, and it may take time and a lot of promotion to stand out.

A more modern approach to passive income is through cryptocurrency staking or yield farming. These can offer high returns but are highly speculative and subject to regulatory changes, security risks, and market volatility.

Creating educational courses or webinars that people can pay to access is a great way to share knowledge while earning. Still, these require frequent updates to remain relevant and there's considerable competition in the e-learning space.

Lastly, practice caution with any vehicle offering quick and easy returns without clear transparency. Solid passive income is built on well-considered investments, not on chasing windfalls.

As with any financial endeavor, diversification is key. Spreading investments across different passive income streams can mitigate risks and provide a more stable income. Remember, some strategies work better together than others; it's all about finding the right balance that suits your risk tolerance, financial goals, and lifestyle. With informed decisions and perseverance, passive income can reinforce a foundation for a secure future.

CHAPTER 11: ONGOING EDUCATION AND FINANCIAL LITERACY

In a world where financial landscapes are ever-evolving, locking in on the pursuit of ongoing education and financial literacy becomes not just an advantage, but a necessity. Let's consider it the intellectual currency that can buy you peace of mind and a sense of preparedness as you navigate through your later years. This chapter aims to cascade not only the significance of keeping your financial knowledge up-to-date but also practical steps on how you can stay informed of the changes and trends that could impact your financial strategy. Empower yourself by tapping into resources for continued learning—diving into books, periodicals, online courses, and workshops that sharpen your financial acumen. Remember, your financial journey isn't static; it's an ongoing process that thrives on informed decisions. Keeping abreast of the latest information and tools ensures you are well-equipped to manage your finances with confidence and agility.

Staying Informed on Financial Changes and Trends

Managing your finances in your prime years demands more than just a static understanding of budgeting and investing. It involves an ongoing commitment to education, particularly about financial changes and trends that could significantly impact your strategy and success. As you've embraced the journey toward financial literacy, this commitment transforms from a daunting task into an empowering habit.

Firstly, it's important to recognize that the financial landscape is always shifting. Interest rates fluctuate, new retirement account regulations emerge, tax laws are updated, and the stock market ebbs and flows due to global events and economic cycles. Staying connected to these changes can assist you in making timely and informed decisions.

One way to stay updated is by routinely checking financial news. This doesn't mean you need to become a day-trader or obsess over stock tickers, but incorporating a review of financial headlines into your daily routine can keep you aware of larger economic trends and topics.

Subscribing to reputable financial newsletters is another powerful tool. They can offer summaries of financial news, professional insights, and actionable advice, tailored to various levels of financial expertise — beginner to advanced. Choosing newsletters that align with your financial goals and reading levels can make financial updates more approachable and less intimidating.

Additionally, podcasts have become an invaluable resource for contemporary financial education. They allow the opportunity to dive deeper into subjects, listen to expert debates, and get explanations on complex issues while you partake in everyday activities like commuting or exercising.

Following thought leaders and financial influencers on social media platforms can also provide quick, digestible insights. But it's critical to verify the credibility of your sources, as the financial advice sphere can sometimes be a breeding ground for misinformation.

Attending seminars and webinars can also enhance your knowledge, and often these events target specific themes like retirement planning, tax strategies, or market analysis. Many of these are free and can provide valuable information in just an hour or two of your time.

Books on financial topics remain one of the most comprehensive resources for deepening your knowledge. Always look out for new releases from reputable authors as they tend to cover current trends and adapting strategies that reflect the latest regulations and market conditions.

It's also worthwhile to periodically review your financial plan in the context of current financial trends. For instance, if there's a downward trend in the housing market and you're contemplating selling property, you might opt to hold off for a while. On the other hand, if interest rates are favorably low, it could be an opportune time to refinance debt.

Enrolling in adult education courses or community college classes that focus on personal finance is an excellent way to both learn about financial trends and receive structured guidance on managing your finances. These courses are typically designed to address a variety of skill levels and often provide hands-on learning experiences.

Joining financial forums and online communities can connect you with peers who are navigating similar financial waters. Such communities often have experienced individuals who offer guidance, and being part of a group can provide moral support and provoke critical thinking about your own financial practices.

Technology, specifically with mobile apps, offers a myriad of tools to keep you abreast of financial news and to manage your personal finances effectively. Budgeting apps, investment tracking, and alert systems for market changes ensure that staying informed is at your fingertips.

Let's not forget the importance of government websites like the IRS or Social Security Administration, which contain a wealth of knowledge about tax laws and retirement benefits. They provide accurate and crucial information that must be part of your financial literacy repertoire.

Lastly, remember that staying informed is not just about reacting to changes in the financial landscape but also about proactively seeking educational opportunities to enhance your financial knowledge. It's a continuous process that, over time, builds confidence in your financial decision-making abilities.

Approach each piece of financial news, each seminar, each podcast, with curiosity and an analytical mind. Question how the information you acquire can directly apply to and benefit your own financial picture. And don't be afraid to make adjustments; the agile learner and investor is often the one who can navigate shifts in the financial tide with grace and confidence.

Think of your financial education as a garden; it needs regular attention, the occasional pruning, and the right nutrients. Stay informed, and you'll cultivate a financial plan that is as robust and resilient as it is fruitful.

Resources for Continued Learning

As you navigate the winding path of financial literacy, the journey doesn't end with the last page of this guide. The landscape of finance continually evolves, and staying abreast of these changes is crucial for your financial well-being. Embarking on ongoing education ensures that your knowledge remains current and your strategies are effective.

To facilitate this continual growth, libraries are a treasure trove of financial wisdom. They often host free workshops, stock the latest financial books, and provide access to premium financial databases. Tap into these resources; they are a springboard for informed decisions.

In the era of the internet, educational websites are only a few clicks away. Websites such as Investopedia, The Simple Dollar, and NerdWallet offer a plethora of articles, glossaries, and tools that can demystify complex financial topics. Remember to scrutinize the information source for credibility to ensure the advice you're receiving is trustworthy.

Podcasts have surged as a powerful medium for learning on the go. Find a financial podcast that resonates with your interests and make it a part of your weekly routine. Hearing from experts and laypeople alike can provide diverse perspectives and stimulate new ideas.

Video tutorials on platforms like YouTube cater to visual learners who absorb information better through watching and listening. Channels dedicated to financial education break down sophisticated concepts into digestible bits that can better your understanding incrementally.

Consider enrolling in online courses. Many universities offer free or low-cost courses on personal finance and investing. MOOCs (Massive Open Online Courses) platforms like Coursera or edX bring Ivy League level education right to your screen.

Don't underestimate the value of community workshops and seminars. These local events not only dispense valuable knowledge but also connect you with like-minded individuals pursuing financial betterment. Such interactions can foster a supportive network and even friendship.

Financial apps can streamline your learning process. They often provide educational resources tailored to their services, which can immensely aid in deepening your understanding of personal finance facets such as budgeting or investing.

Books on personal finance should be a staple in your ongoing education. Whether they address the psychological approach to money or tangible strategies for wealth accumulation, there's a breadth of literature that can complement any learning style and preference. As financial paradigms shift, update your home library with new thought-provoking titles.

Subscribe to financial journals and magazines such as "The Wall Street Journal," "Bloomberg Businessweek," or "Kiplinger's Personal Finance". These publications can provide high-quality, up-to-date information on market trends and economic insights that can influence your financial plans.

Always have a reliable benchmark for financial news, ensuring you can assess the impact of economic changes on your assets and strategies. Establishing a regimen of checking key financial news sources daily can keep you ahead of the curve.

Joining finance-related groups and forums online can be a fountain of knowledge and support. Sites like Reddit's personal finance communities or Facebook finance groups are filled with real-life experiences, Q&A sessions, and moral support from peers who are also refining their financial acumen.

Webinars and live streams conducted by financial experts offer an interactive way to learn and pose questions that are specific to your personal financial situation. Many financial institutions and advisory services host these virtual events, often free of charge.

Mentorship can be incredibly valuable — seek out individuals who have navigated their own financial journeys successfully. They can provide bespoke advice, learned through experience, which can be instrumental in avoiding pitfalls and capitalizing on opportunities.

Lastly, make use of government resources like the Consumer Financial Protection Bureau (CFPB), which provides a wealth of information to help you make smarter financial decisions. Taking advantage of these resources can guide you towards a more secure and prosperous financial future.

By supplementing your financial journey with these resources, you pave the way for a lifetime of learning and self-improvement. Embrace the attitude that knowledge is the fuel of financial success, and let it drive you towards the bright future you deserve.

CHAPTER 12: FINANCIAL ADVISORS AND PROFESSIONAL HELP

As we journey further into the heart of financial rejuvenation, the path becomes more complex and the stakes higher; it's here that the expertise of financial advisors and professional help becomes invaluable. Navigating the ever-evolving financial landscape requires a keen eye and an experienced hand, especially when the time to recover from missteps is not on your side. A trustworthy financial advisor is not just a guide but a partner in sculpting a future that's as secure as it is rewarding. In identifying when the complexity of your financial situation necessitates this level of assistance, you'll be taking a critical step toward empowerment. Moreover, selecting the right advisor—one who aligns with your goals, understands your unique circumstances, and emboldens you to take control of your financial destiny—is a decision that can richly enhance the tapestry of your later years. Embark on this chapter to uncover the pivotal moments that signal the need for professional support and learn how to discern the caliber of advisor that best suits the future you envision.

When to Seek Professional Financial Advice

As you journey through the maze of personal finance after your 40s, you may find yourself at a crossroads, figuring out whether to turn left toward self-guidance, or right, seeking the wisdom of a professional financial advisor. It's a pivotal decision, one that can influence the trajectory of your financial health and future security.

Firstly, consider professional financial advice when life throws a curveball that complicates your financial picture. This might include receiving an inheritance, going through a divorce, or facing a sudden health crisis. These events can alter your fiscal landscape, and a seasoned professional can help navigate the terrain.

Another crucial time is when you're approaching retirement. If you're unsure how to maximize your retirement savings or convert your nest egg into a steady retirement income, it's wise to consult a financial advisor. They can help optimize your assets for the golden years ahead, ensuring you can retire comfortably and sustainably.

If you're feeling overwhelmed with investment options, it might be time to look for help. With loads of investment vehicles out there—from stocks and bonds to mutual funds and ETFs—choosing the right mix for your portfolio can be daunting. Financial advisors can assess your risk tolerance and financial goals, crafting an investment strategy tailor-made for you.

What if you're struggling to pay off debt? If high-interest debt has become an albatross around your neck, a financial professional can assist in exploring strategies such as consolidation or refinancing, which can simplify repayments and potentially lower interest rates.

Some life goals, like education funding for children or buying a home later in life, come with complex financial implications. An advisor can help you understand these financial commitments and weigh them against other savings and investment priorities.

Moreover, if you're finding it challenging to keep up with the ever-changing tax laws and how they affect your investments, it's perhaps time to consult a professional. Advisors stay current on tax reforms and can provide guidance on tax-efficient investing and estate planning.

Another indication that you might need professional advice is when you lack the time or inclination to manage your finances diligently. If you're too busy with career, family, or other obligations, delegating to a financial advisor can help you stay on track without sacrificing your valuable time.

If you've amassed a sizeable estate and are concerned about legacy planning, it is prudent to reach out for professional advice. An advisor can work with you to devise strategies for wealth transfer, philanthropic endeavors, and ensuring your assets are managed as per your wishes after you're gone.

Are you starting to think about a business venture or a career transition? These decisions come with financial implications. An advisor can provide a objective analysis and strategic insights that align with your financial objectives.

Also, if you're simply looking for confirmation that you're on the right path, an expert opinion can offer reassurance or alert you to overlooked opportunities or risks. It's like a financial health checkup—it never hurts to ensure everything's in working order.

Perhaps you have specific financial questions or you find yourself guessing when making financial decisions. Guesswork can be costly in finance, and the expertise of a financial advisor can transform doubts into informed decisions.

Let's not overlook those who've managed their finances solo but who, with advancing age, wish to ensure continuity of financial management in case they can no longer do it themselves. Establishing a relationship with a financial advisor now can provide a seamless transition when necessary.

Navigating the complexities of financial products such as annuities, life insurance, and long-term care insurance may also impel you to seek advice. Advisors can demystify the fine print and help you understand how these products could fit into your overall financial plan.

Finally, if you're contemplating making charitable contributions effectively, an advisor can guide you through the various options and the potential tax advantages, ensuring their alignment with your broader financial goals.

In conclusion, the question of when to seek professional financial advice doesn't have a one-size-fits-all answer. It's a personal decision that depends on your unique financial circumstances, goals, and comfort level with managing money. However, recognizing when you could benefit from professional insight is critical. It can mean the difference between a financial strategy that's just adequate and one that's exceptional, propelling you toward a future of financial confidence and stability.

Selecting the Right Financial Advisor for You

Embarking on the journey of financial rejuvenation after 40 can be both exhilarating and intimidating. As your path unfurls before you, replete with goals and the will to achieve them, the pursuit often necessitates a sage companion: a financial advisor. Not just any advisor, but one who is tailored to your unique situation, understands your late start, and propels you towards a secure future.

Finding the appropriate advisor is akin to selecting a partner for a marathon. This individual will not only offer advice but also shape your financial mindset and strategy. You'll need someone with the experience to navigate complex financial waters and the foresight to help you avoid potential pitfalls ahead.

Begin with clarity on what you seek from a financial advisor. Are they to provide comprehensive planning, or focus on investment management? Perhaps your need is for specific advice on retirement planning or estate planning? Understanding these needs will direct your search and ensure alignment with the advisor's expertise.

Verify credentials, as they are hallmarks of an advisor's commitment to their profession. Look for certifications such as CFP® (Certified Financial Planner), which indicates a well-rounded financial education and adherence to ethical standards. Similarly, other designations can also reflect specialization in areas like retirement planning or wealth management.

Consider the advisor's investment philosophy. It should resonate with your risk tolerance and investment horizon. Whether they advocate for active or passive investment strategies, it is essential that their approach aligns with your goals and comfort level with risk.

Don't shy away from discussing fees upfront. Financial advisors can employ various compensation models, from fee-only structures to commissions on products they sell. Understand these models, and seek transparency to ensure their recommendations are not driven by the prospect of a higher commission.

Interview multiple advisors. This process is not just about evaluating qualifications, but also about finding someone you can trust and communicate with effectively. Pay attention to how well they listen and whether they can convey complex information in an understandable manner.

Assess their track record. A seasoned advisor should be able to provide examples of how they've helped others in similar situations. While past performance isn't an indicator of future results, their history can reveal much about their professionalism and consistency.

Reputation matters immensely in this delicate arena. Research the potential advisors online, looking for testimonials and reviews. A clean regulatory history and high professional standing speak volumes.

Proximity may also be a factor. Some prefer face-to-face meetings and a local presence, while others are comfortable with virtual interactions. Decide what works best for you, considering that a solid relationship often benefits from personal interaction.

Inquire about the services offered. Will they assist with tax planning, estate planning, or insurance needs? An advisor who offers a broad range of services can help you view your finances as a cohesive whole, rather than isolated silos requiring individual attention.

Leverage referrals from friends or colleagues who also embarked on financial improvement later in life. They can provide candid insights about their advisors – both the victories and the challenges.

Prepare to make a commitment. Once you select an advisor, forge a partnership that is more than transactional. Be prepared to work closely with them, providing full disclosure of your financial life to get the most tailored advice.

Finally, monitor and evaluate the relationship regularly. Just like any other aspect of your financial journey, the advisor's performance should be periodically reviewed to ensure it meets your evolving needs and expectations.

Selecting the right financial advisor is a vital step towards solidifying your financial future. Identifying a fiduciary who puts your interests first, working in unison with you, can help turn your financial dreams into attainable goals. The effort put into this choice can reward you with wisdom, confidence, and peace of mind as you navigate through your prime years towards a fulfilling retirement.

BUILDING A LEGACY OF FINANCIAL STABILITY

As we draw this guide to a close, let's reflect on the journey we've embarked upon together. The path to financial stability, particularly when you're getting a later start, is strewn with challenges and opportunities alike. But as you now understand, it's never too late to take control of your finances and build the legacy you desire. You've gained the tools and wisdom necessary to navigate the complexities of your financial landscape with confidence and poise.

Through understanding your financial starting point and setting realistic goals, you have laid the foundation upon which your financial house can be securely built. Crafting a sustainable budget has become an art form you are now well-practiced in, able to prioritize expenses and discern where cuts can be beneficial. Not only have you come to appreciate the importance of saving, both for the immediate future and the long haul, but you are actively engaged in the process.

Debt, once a daunting obstacle, is now a challenge you face head-on with strategic precision. You've learned to identify and avoid common debt traps, and have tackled high-interest debts with smart and calculated techniques. Investing, too, is no longer a realm reserved for the mystically finance-savvy; you've grasped investment fundamentals and recognize the importance of retirement accounts and late-start investments, understanding the nuisances of IRAs, 401(k)s, and annuities.

Home ownership decisions in later life, be it buying or renting, have become clearer as you've learned to manage mortgages and home equity to your advantage. Insurance, which often presents a complex maze of options and decisions, has become a system you can navigate to ensure your health and legacy are protected through informed choices that best serve your personal situation.

Your retirement planning is robust, built with an accurate estimation of your retirement needs, and bolstered by strategic catch-up contributions and tax considerations. Estate planning, once a distant concept, is now firmly within your grasp, with a will established, and trusts, healthcare directives, and powers of attorney set in place to safeguard your intentions.

In your quest for financial stability, the creation of passive income streams has emerged as a powerful tool. You have learned to identify opportunities and weigh the risks against the potential rewards, working diligently to create additional sources of income that complement your active efforts.

Recognizing the vital importance of ongoing education and financial literacy, you've committed to staying informed on financial changes and trends. The landscape of finance is ever-evolving, and your dedication to continued learning places you in a position of strength and adaptability.

When the complexities of finance have required expertise beyond your current knowledge, you've learned when and how to seek professional financial advice. Selecting the right financial advisor for your unique situation is a decision you now approach with clarity and confidence.

The final message to take with you is one of hope and encouragement. Your financial journey is unique and personal, filled with its singular blend of challenges and triumphs. But the steps you've taken, the knowledge you've absorbed, and the actions you've implemented form the bedrock of a stable and promising financial future.

Achieving financial stability is an ongoing process, one that demands persistence, education, and adaptability. The journey doesn't end with the last page of this book—it's a continuous evolution, where each day provides a fresh opportunity to fortify your legacy. Every decision you make, every dollar you save, every debt you reduce, and every investment you nurture contributes to the mosaic of your financial well-being.

As you progress, remember that your legacy is not just about the assets you'll leave behind; it's equally about the values you instill, the habits you foster, and the example you set for those who might one day follow in your footsteps. Financial stability is as much about imparting wisdom as it is about accumulating wealth. It's about creating a foundation that not only stands the test of time but also empowers others to build upon it.

Look back at your accomplishments with pride and look forward to the future with a vision. No goal is too lofty when you approach it with a sound strategy and a steadfast commitment. Your dedication thus far has shown that, even in the face of adversity, you can rise and triumph.

Now, as you close this book, don't close the chapter on your financial growth. Embrace the future with the same passion and determination that brought you to this point. Building a legacy of financial stability is a journey worth every step, every sacrifice, and every triumph. Your legacy awaits.

APPENDIX A: FINANCIAL PLANNING WORKSHEETS AND TOOLS

Embarking on a journey to financial health can indeed be a transformative experience. Now that you've delved into the intricate world of personal finance, you are well on your way to securing a brighter, more stable future for yourself. It's a hefty challenge but one that is entirely within your reach. That's where this appendix comes in. Financial planning worksheets and tools are the tangible resources you can utilize to track progress, stay focused, and truly make your financial plans resonate with your day-to-day life.

Net Worth Calculator

Your personal balance sheet is a reflection of where you stand financially. We'll begin by laying out a simple yet comprehensive sheet to calculate your net worth. This encompasses all your assets such as savings, retirement accounts, real estate values, and personal property, while subtracting your liabilities, including loans, mortgages, and other debts. By keeping this up-to-date, you'll have a clear snapshot of your financial health at any moment.

Budget Planner

Living without a budget is like navigating a ship without a map. You might eventually get somewhere, but you will have no idea when or what condition you'll be in upon arrival. A thorough budget planner is vital and will be your day-to-day guide. You'll categorize your income and expenses, separating needs from wants, and truly understand where every dollar is going. Being hands-on with your finances heightens awareness and fosters responsible spending habits.

Debt Repayment Plan

Dealing with debt requires a battle strategy – your debt repayment plan is just that. Identify all your current debts, list their interest rates, and develop a prioritized repayment schedule. Often, the 'avalanche' or 'snowball' methods are used to systematically eliminate debts, and you'll find steps to applying these methods to your own circumstances.

Emergency Fund Tracker

An emergency fund isn't merely a buffer – it's your financial lifeline in times of unexpected events. This tool will help you determine the desired size of your emergency fund and track contributions. Regular monitoring can inspire you to reach that goal quicker, providing you with peace of mind.

Investment Portfolio Overview

Sage investment decisions are key to growing your wealth. Whether you're new to investing or not, an investment portfolio overview sheet will help you keep track of your various investments, their performance, and how they align with your risk tolerance and time horizon. By reassessing your investments periodically, you'll be well-positioned to make informed decisions.

Retirement Planning Worksheet

It's never too late to start planning for retirement, and the sooner you define your retirement goals, the better. This worksheet will enable you to outline your retirement timeline, estimate expenses, determine income needs, and understand how different savings vehicles such as IRAs and 401(k)s fit into your plan.

Estate Planning Checklist

Estate planning is more than just allocating your assets after you pass away—it's about making sure your wishes are known and honored. This checklist will guide you through the essentials like wills, trusts, healthcare directives, and power of attorney. It's a roadmap to ensure your legacy is built exactly as you envision.

By utilizing these worksheets and tools, you can embark on a methodical and informed financial journey. They will serve as grounding instruments, guiding your path, and ensuring you remain disciplined and proactive about your financial health. Keep these tools updated; refer to them often, and remember, they are instruments of empowerment, designed to help you sculpt a future filled with stability and promise.

With these practical and effective resources at hand, you're not just planning for your future; you're actively building it. Allow yourself to dream large, set ambitious goals, and take consistent, calculated steps towards them. The path to financial recovery and growth is a path of empowerment, resilience, and ultimately, a testament to the human spirit's capacity for renewal.

Glossary of Financial Terms

Embarking on a financial journey, especially when the sands of time have gathered, can be as daunting as it is crucial. To aid in traversing the landscape of money management and investment, having a command on the language of finance is indispensable. Whether you're deciphering the twists and turns of mortgage rates or engaging with the complexities of retirement plans, this glossary serves as your beacon through the fog of financial jargon. Let's illuminate these terms, equipping you with the confidence to pilot your fiscal future with acumen and grace.

A

- **Annuities:** A form of insurance or investment entailing a series of payments made at equal intervals. Conceived for retirements, annuities guarantee income for a specified period or for life.
- **Assets:** Anything of value owned by an individual or entity. Assets can include cash, investments, property, and more, each bolstering one's financial standing.

B

- **Budget:** A financial plan for a specific period, often structuring spending and saving. Drafting a budget is pivotal in charting one's financial course, identifying what you can spend while still sailing towards your savings horizon.

- **Bond:** A fixed-income instrument representing a loan made by an investor to a borrower. A dependable way to diversify one's portfolio, bonds can bestow a predictable income stream.

C

- **Compound Interest:** The interest on a loan or deposit calculated based on both the initial principal and the accumulated interest from previous periods. It's interest earned upon interest, a potent force in the world of finance that can magnify wealth over time.
- **Credit Score:** A numerical expression representing the creditworthiness of an individual, predictive of the likelihood to repay debts. A sturdy credit score isn't just a number—it's a golden key to favorable loan conditions.

D

- **Debt Consolidation:** The act of taking out a new loan to pay off other liabilities and consumer debts, generally unsecured ones. This technique can streamline multiple debts into a single, systematic payment.
- **Diversification:** A risk management strategy that mixes a wide variety of investments within a portfolio. Diversification may smooth out investment returns, as one is not overly exposed to any single asset or risk.

E

- **Emergency Fund:** A dedicated savings account set aside to cover unexpected life events, such as job loss or medical emergencies. It isn't merely a fund; it's fortifying your financial future against unforeseen acts of fate.

- **Equity:** In real estate, equity refers to the difference between the property's current market value and the mortgage amount still owed. In the broader financial sense, it signifies ownership interest in a company through common or preferred stock.

I

- **IRA (Individual Retirement Account):** A tax-advantaged investing tool for individuals to earmark funds for retirement savings. Whether it's a Traditional or a Roth IRA, these accounts can be lynchpins in a retirement plan's foundation.
- **Income Stream:** A regular flow of money from employment, investments, or other sources. Multiple income streams can diversify one's inflow, buffering against job loss or economic downturns.

M

- **Mortgage:** A loan typically used to purchase a home where the property serves as collateral. Understanding the terms of a mortgage—the interest rate, term, and payment schedule—is vital for homeownership.
- **Mutual Funds:** An investment program funded by shareholders that trades in diversified holdings and is managed by professional money managers. It's a way to pool your resources with others, aiming for a collective financial gain.

P

- **Portfolio:** A range of investments held by an individual or institution. A thoughtfully composed portfolio is a canvas displaying your financial strategy and risk tolerance.

- **Principal:** The initial size of a loan, or the amount of money invested. Paying down the principal can speed up debt reduction and foster faster equity growth.

R

- **Retirement Accounts:** Financial accounts (such as 401(k)s, IRAs, and pension plans) designed to support individuals in their retirement years. These accounts often come with tax advantages, reinforcing your long-term financial bulwark.
- **Roth IRA:** An individual retirement account allowing after-tax contributions to grow tax-free. When the time for retirement dispersal arrives, the bounty can be plucked without succumbing to taxation.

S

- **Savings Account:** A deposit account held at a financial institution that provides principal security and a modest interest rate. An essential thread in the fabric of a sound savings strategy.
- **Stock:** A type of security that signifies ownership in a corporation and represents a claim on part of the corporation's assets and earnings. There are two main types of stock: common and preferred.

T

- **Tax Deduction:** A deduction that lowers a person's tax liability by lowering his taxable income. Effective use of tax deductions requires strategic planning but can significantly reduce one's annual tax burden.

Armed with this glossary, you now have a sturdy keel to keep your financial ship steady, even in uncharted waters. Remember, knowledge is the beacon that guides you to safe harbor. Each term you master is a step towards building a legacy of financial stability—a testament to foresight and wisdom.

APPENDIX B: FURTHER READING AND RESOURCES

As we close the pages of this essential guide, let's remember that the journey towards financial proficiency doesn't end here. The world of personal finance is vast and ever-changing, and staying informed is crucial to maintaining and improving your financial health. In this appendix, you'll find a curated list of further reading and resources that will enhance your understanding, keep you updated, and inspire continued progress in your financial life.

Books for Financial Enlightenment

To deepen your knowledge beyond the scope of this guide, consider delving into books that cover various aspects of financial planning, budgeting, saving, and investing. These books have been selected for their accessibility and relevance to improving your financial life, especially in the later stages:

- *Smart Couples Finish Rich*: This book equips you with techniques to collaborate with your partner on crafting a secure financial future.
- *Your Money or Your Life*: A compelling read that challenges you to transform your relationship with money and achieve financial independence.
- *The Total Money Makeover*: A step-by-step guide for those looking to take control of their finances and work towards debt freedom and financial peace.

Online Resources and Tools

Online tools and resources are ideal for keeping pace with the dynamic world of personal finance. Here are some of the most reliable and user-friendly websites to explore:

- The official **IRS Website** (irs.gov) can be invaluable when you need clarity on tax-related questions, especially regarding retirement accounts and catch-up contributions.
- Websites like **Morningstar** (morningstar.com) or **Investopedia** (investopedia.com) provide extensive investment insights and educational content suitable for both beginners and experienced investors.
- For budgeting and tracking your finances, apps such as **Mint** (mint.com) or **Personal Capital** (personalcapital.com) are highly recommended.

Podcasts and Video Channels

For those who prefer listening to advice or watching financial commentary, here's a concise list of podcasts and video channels that stand out for their quality content:

- The *Retirement Answer Man* podcast focuses on retirement planning and provides practical advice for those getting a later start.
- *Money for the Rest of Us* is another podcast that teaches how money works, how to invest it, and how to live without worrying about it.
- YouTube channels such as **The Financial Diet** and **Graham Stephan** offer engaging videos on personal finance and investing topics.

Professional Organizations and Groups

Joining professional organizations can provide you with not just networking opportunities, but also workshops, seminars, and publications to broaden your knowledge. Consider the following:

- National Association of Personal Financial Advisors (NAPFA): **A leading association of fee-only financial advisors.**
- **American Association of Individual Investors (AAII)**: Provides tools and education to help individual investors make informed investment decisions.
- Local investment or financial planning clubs that meet regularly can offer support and shared learning among peers.

Taking these steps to expand your financial literacy can have a transformative effect on your financial stability and peace of mind. The resources listed here are starting points—keep exploring, inquiring, and learning. Remember, the dedication you show today shapes the security and prosperity of your tomorrow.

Scan for Other Books by The Author

To enrich your journey towards financial empowerment, explore other titles by the author that delve into a wide array of topics designed to fortify your knowledge, inspire action, and drive you towards a future brimming with possibility and security.

www.ingramcontent.com/pod-product-compliance
Lightning Source LLC
LaVergne TN
LVHW100329210926
848480LV00003B/1296

* 9 7 8 1 9 2 3 4 5 2 2 8 2 *